Pleyn Delit: Medieval Cookery for Modern Cooks

Constance B. Hieatt & Sharon Butler

Pleyn Delit

Medieval Cookery for Modern Cooks

University of Toronto Press
Toronto Buffalo London

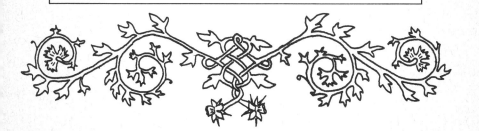

FOR OUR MOTHERS

© University of Toronto Press 1976
Toronto Buffalo London
Printed in Canada
Revised and reprinted 1979
First paperback edition 1979

Library of Congress Cataloging in Publication Data

Hieatt, Constance B
Pleyn delit.

Bibliography: p. 161
Includes index.
1. Cookery. I. Butler, Sharon, 1942-
joint author. II. Title.
TX652.H53   641.5   76-29734
ISBN 0-8020-2252-9
ISBN 0-8020-6366-7 pbk.

This book has been published
with the assistance of grants from the
Canada Council and the
Ontario Arts Council.

Contents

Preface

The idea for this book was born some six years ago, and gradually took form more clearly as we worked, on and off, testing recipes – sometimes together, sometimes independently, sometimes with others assisting. Constance Hieatt carried out most of the library research, on this continent and in England, as a sort of intermezzo sandwiched between other scholarly errands. Sharon Butler has done all the art work. The diverting chore of working out and testing recipes was shared, as was the writing.

We owe an incalculable debt to fellow cooks who have worked with our recipes over the years, especially Brenda Thaon and Brian Shaw. The adventurous trenchermen whose judicious comments were helpful are legion, but Paul Thaon deserves special mention, as do A. Kent Hieatt and John Lingard. We have reason to be grateful to various members of the staff of the University of Toronto Press for enthusiastic guidance and assistance: without Prudence Tracy's editorial acumen and Allan Fleming's talents as a designer the final result could never have been so pleasing to its authors.

But our most basic debt is to our mothers, who guided our early steps in the kitchen.

CBH SB

Introduction

A FRANKELEYN was in his compaignye.
Whit was his berd as is the dayes eye;
Of his complexioun he was sangwyn.
Wel loved he by the morwe a sop in wyn;
To lyven in delit was evere his wone,
For he was Epicurus owene sone,
That heeld opinioun that pleyn delit
Was verray felicitee parfit.

from the General Prologue to The Canterbury Tales

In the last decade or so a great many people, only a few of them students of the middle ages, have become intrigued with the idea of banqueting medieval-style; anyone who has travelled, or read tourist literature and advertisements, must know by now that medieval fare is available, and consumed at considerable cost, in an Irish castle, an expensive London restaurant, and other successful commercial establishments in Britain and the European continent. In both Britain and North America medieval 'feasts' are being held with ever increasing frequency, not only in academic communities but as church suppers and the like. Yet there has never been, and still is not, a medieval cookbook which could be safely used by anyone but an expert in Middle English with a great deal of experience as a cook. This book is intended to fill that gap.

Such medieval cookbooks as have been available fall into three rough categories. The first, and most useful because most complete, includes various scholarly editions of fourteenth and fifteenth century cookery rolls. The best-known of these is the *Two Fifteenth Century Cookery Books* published by the Early English Text Society.[1] Such editions were intended as background information for scholars specializing in the period, and certainly not to be used as cookbooks. The modern reader who wishes to turn such books to kitchen use is on his own in deciding how much of this or that to use, and often even to determine what the general effect should be: editors have been somewhat unreliable guides. A second category might be termed the coffee-table variety, intended to amuse and beguile, but rarely to be much use in the kitchen. Such books have tended to emphasize the exotic, and sometimes even to discourage readers from trying to cook the recipes presented. A third, if slightly overlapping, category is that of the historical cookbooks which present a selection of medieval recipes 'adapted' for modern tastes. Their selections are also often slanted towards the stranger and more exotic dishes, frequently so drastically adapted as to be a long way from authenticity. They invariably provide only a slender sampling of the fare of the period.

Our aim, then, has not been that of any previous editor. We intended to produce a large and representative collection for practical use in the kitchen, not — or not just — in the study or living room, for those who may enjoy recreating their culinary heritage on either a grand or a modest scale. Whether one wishes to give a do-it-yourself Medieval Feast or simply to vary the everyday repertoire, much can be learned from the medieval cooks whose notes were collected in the manuscripts from which we have drawn. The most cautious and conservative cook should find here appealingly economical and simple fare; the gourmet can discover something to titillate the most jaded palate. Even seasoned medievalists are likely to be surprised at the full range of the cookery of the period, a matter which has been sadly misunderstood. It is not nearly so difficult as most scholars assume or so displeasing to modern tastes, to reproduce the epicurean 'pleyn delit' which characterized Chaucer's Franklin's bounteous table.

Recipes selected for this volume are first given in their original form, though we have sometimes emended the punctuation, and, in the case of those taken from French sources, translated into English. Comments follow, where they seemed necessary or helpful; anyone interested in authenticity may

thus compare and judge for himself the accuracy of the recipes below, given in standard modern kitchen terms. All our
directions have been thoroughly kitchen-tested, except for a
few variants which are appended for the reader's edification
and amusement. Not that amusement is our primary purpose:
nor even edification, in a truly scholarly sense.[2] Yet a certain
amount of both, especially edification, is certainly desirable.
For one thing, the number of still circulating misconceptions
about the food of the period, even (even perhaps especially)
among medievalists, is deplorable.

Almost everyone who has written on the subject has suggested that medieval people preferred rich, spicy foods
drowned in outlandish sauces, and that they never ate simple
fare, especially vegetables and salads, unless forced to by pov-
erty. These and other commonplaces are simply false. Much
medieval cooking was so bland as to seem dull today. Spices,
to judge by extant household records of a year's supply, not
to mention cost, were no doubt used as sparingly as a modern
cook uses pepper: when a dish is meant to be strongly flavoured with a particular spice, the directions call for 'a great
deal of ...' Logically, then, unless a 'great deal' is called for,
frugality was the rule. The argument that many and lavish
spices were necessary because so much meat and fish was
salted down for the winter is unconvincing. Salt fish or meat
can be soaked (or parboiled, as is frequently called for in
medieval recipes) until it loses all its salty quality – which is
not necessarily desirable.

Rich dishes in exotic sauces appear to be in the minority on
actual medieval menus. The most elaborate multi-course feasts
had a higher proportion of roasts and plain boiled meats,
served with simple 'pottages' of vegetables, than of fancier
dishes. And far more vegetables were grown and used, alone
or in combination with meat, eggs, or fish, than is generally
recognized: the treatises on gardening list dozens of varieties,
often differentiating between those which should be cooked
and those suitable for salads. The post-medieval revolution in
tastes and cooking habits assumed by writers in this area is,
we suspect, more a matter of emphases than of basic tastes

x and techniques. Many foods and flavourings which are ubiquitous today (such as tomatoes, coffee, and vanilla) had not yet been introduced into the British and European kitchen, and thus it is natural that more use was made of other available ingredients. But there has been much more continuity than has been realized.

'Green sauce,' for example, appears in accounts of European food at least as early as the twelfth century and was a standard favourite with fish throughout the period, and later: a recipe of around the turn of the seventeenth century is virtually identical with those of earlier centuries, and the same sauce is still served in modern France, and probably elsewhere, with only slight modifications. Almost everything which seems odd to British and North American tastes has modern descendants somewhere in European cuisine. Even the practice of 'gilding' poultry, and, sometimes, then replacing the feathered hide intact, has been reported to us from several quarters.

Some of the common misconceptions about medieval food are easily traceable to misunderstanding of the evidence presented by the cookery rolls and by the menus which have come down to us from various state occasions or as sample 'model' menus. Actually, when the two sources of evidence are placed side by side, they contradict (or supplement) each other in various ways. The idea that roasted meats, aside from poultry, were rare in the period goes back to Pegge, one of the early editors, who interpreted the preponderance of stews over roasts in the manuscripts as meaning that fewer roasts were consumed. But it is precisely because roasting is a simple, common procedure that no one would have thought it necessary to write down directions for performing it; knowledge of roasting procedures is assumed in some of the more elaborate recipes, which may tell us to roast the spiced meatballs, or sausages in the form of porcupines, or whatever, 'as one does pigs,' or something of the sort. And if Pegge had looked further into the recipe rolls he would have found a goodly number of recipes for sauces to accompany plain roasts. But also, as we have remarked above, menus for feasts

on grand state occasions show a far greater proportion of
roasts of various kinds than of more elaborate dishes. Even
the wedding feast of Henry IV offered such items as 'gross
char' – a large roast of meat so un-aristocratic, in comparison
with game, as not to deserve more precise description: probably this was roast beef, if it was to be really 'gross.'

The aristocratic menu, on the other hand, is misleading in
giving very few clear references to vegetables, and, as far as
we know, none at all to salads. There may have been a good
many vegetables lurking in the various pottages and other
dishes. The recipe rolls, which generally claim to emanate
from the royalty or the higher nobility, include many recipes
for simple vegetable dishes. Further, the various warnings
against eating salads and raw fruits, which have been cited as
proof that they were not eaten, prove quite the opposite:
who bothers to condemn a non-existent practice?

The menus also show a greater sense of order in the serving
of a multi-course meal than has usually been perceived. A
typical English feast menu for days on which meat was permissible started with pork (or boar) served with mustard or
pepper sauce and either bacon with pease pottage or venison
with frumenty, which were invariable combinations. The re-
mainder of the first course consisted of the more common
roasts or boiled meats with, usually, one meat pie or pasty.
Two other courses generally followed on state occasions, in
each of which more roasts appeared, usually featuring game
birds, along with more complicated pottages of meats, poultry, and fish in various sauces; the last course was usually the
richest, with more pastries, fried dishes such as fritters, jellies,
and sweetened foods than occur in earlier courses. The same
general order prevails in the menus for fish days, which almost
invariably begin with red – smoked and/or pickled – herring:
still the standard way to begin a meal in Scandinavia and
hardly unknown elsewhere.

Thus it seems apparent that menu-planners followed the
advice which can be found in various sources to start with the
plainer foods and eat the delicacies afterwards. A last course
of fruit, nuts, wafers, and other small delicacies is not often

mentioned on English menus, but would appear to have been part of the normal routine, perhaps so much so that this was not thought worth noting on the menu of a major feast any more than was bread, which is never mentioned on any menu but was the indispensable part of any meal, simple or complex. In general, the French menu was much like those recorded in England except that the first course was often composed of pastries and elegant concoctions, with the plainer roasts postponed to the second course. Thus the French were already tending to give diners 'appetizers' before the more solid part of the meal.

It may well be asked what relation feast menus have to everyday eating. Probably the main meal of the day, a midday or late morning dinner, was a fairly lavish one in an aristocratic household, consisting of the equivalent of at least the first course of a feast menu. This would appear to be the model emulated by the bourgeoisie and country squires such as Chaucer's Franklin. Most people, of course, would have had to settle for rather less. In the case of the peasantry, we may note that the poor widow of the Nun's Priest's Tale subsisted almost entirely on bread and milk, with bacon and a few eggs to add variety. In a period of drought Piers Plowman complained that he did not even have any bacon – just some fresh cheese, the coarsest types of bread, and a supply of herbs and greens; but his almost equally poor neighbours responded by bringing gifts of peas, beans, fruits, and onions. Servants in a household of any standing did much better than that. The Ménagier de Paris admonished his young wife to be sure that her servants got the proper food and drink, and the morning breakfast order for the nursery given in an early sixteenth century source specifies a quart of beer and three boiled mutton bones to feed the nurse and her two infant charges; in Lent, of course, fish was substituted for the meat.

The lord and lady of the manor ate a really hearty breakfast. Between them, they were to be served one loaf of bread sliced into 'trenchers' – the medieval equivalent of plates; two small loaves of higher quality bread; a quart of beer; a quart of wine; and a good-sized piece of beef or boiled mutton. Yet

we gather from Chaucer that a true gourmet's breakfast consisted simply of toast and wine: both the Franklin and Janu-
ary, the elderly knight of the Merchant's Tale, broke their
fasts of a morning with a 'sop in wine.' Supper, the third
meal of the day, consisted of dishes similar to those served
for dinner, though probably in smaller quantities. Some of
the feast menus combine dinner and supper, obviously suggesting that the party took time off from eating for other
pastimes between courses, but also suggesting that supper
menus may have featured less hearty, more 'delicate' foods.

Perhaps the best example of the kind of fare which 'snowed'
upon the Franklin's table is a model menu given in John Russell's *Boke of Nurture* for a 'Feast for a Franklin.' The first
course consists of 'brawn' (cold pork?) with mustard, bacon
with pease pottage, stewed beef or mutton, boiled chicken or
capon, roast goose or pork, and a capon pie or 'crustard' (a
tart resembling a modern quiche): a total of six dishes, mostly
simple ones. The second course started with either 'mortrewes' – ground meat or fish in a bland mixture nearer to
soup than to paté in consistency – or a sort of savoury pudding made with bread crumbs, then went on to roasts: veal or
lamb, kid or rabbit, chicken or pigeon; and some sort of meat
pie or pasty. After this came fritters and mixtures thick
enough to be served in slices. The feast was to end with apples
and pears (possibly baked) with spices; bread and cheese;
and, finally, spiced cakes and wafers, served with spiced ale
and mead.

More aristocratic menus differ only in the number of dishes
served and the substitution of spiced wine for spiced ale and
mead. However, there was one more indispensable feature of
feasts for great occasions: the 'subtlety' (usually spelled 'Sotil-
tee') which provided the climax of every course. Most festive
subtilties appear to have been made of sugar, no doubt com-
bined with other things, and were the sort of confectionary
art that survives today in fancy cake decorations, especially
the bride and groom which traditionally stand at the top of a
wedding cake. Our ancestors had different ideas of suitable
motifs for a wedding feast: the high point of one such occa-

sion was a subtlety showing 'a wyf lying in childe-bed,' an obvious hint to the bride. Many subtleties appear to have been figures of birds or animals, often bearing suitable mottos, but they sometimes ran to minature castles or cathedrals, or figures of saints or of the dignitaries being honoured. One of the more intriguing known ones depicted Father, Son, and Holy Ghost in Trinity, which sounds like a pretty tricky job for the pastry cook. (See the appendix on subtleties.)

In our own menu planning we have tended to follow the French model when we have given feasts, since it lends itself to an order familiar to modern diners. For smaller meals, the English style is quite suitable, since there is always a simple pottage at or near the beginning of a meal – a tradition which lingers on in the archetypal English dinner today. We hope readers will scan the varied possibilities and put together their own menus according to their tastes and pocketbooks, but the menus which follow provide examples of combinations we found pleasing to various guests. (The quantities given with each recipe are sufficient to feed 4 to 6 people.)

1 *A simple but elegant dinner for 4-6*
Cold Chicken Livers (35)
Chicken with Orange Sauce (82), served with crusty bread
Salad (44)
Cream Junket with Blueberries (108)

2 *A gourmet meal for 4-6*
Green Almond Soup (2)
Chicken and Shellfish in Shellfish Sauce (104) with
    bread or rice and Peapods (41)
Cheese Custard Tart (118, var. 2)

3 *A dinner for 8-12*
(double all quantities)
Oysters Stewed in Ale (7)
Mushroom Pasties (24)
Pork in Pepper Sauce (94), with Braised Spinach (40) and
    Barley (22, var.)
Apple Fritters (119)

4 *A feast for about 20*

(some quantities should be doubled)

To be placed on the table before guests are seated: bread, butter, wine

Hors d'œuvres: Brie Tarts (23), Shrimps (26), Gilded Meatballs with Currants (28, var. 2)

Main dishes and side dishes: Roast Beef with Garlic Pepper Sauce (70); Chicken in White Wine Sauce (84); Salmon and Leeks in Almond Sauce (50); Kidney Stew (103); Noodles (45); Buttered Greens (22); Green Peas (19); Parsnip Fritters (39)

Dessert: Strawberry Pudding (107); Apple Tarts (116); Sweet Fritters (121); Nuts (preferably glazed or spiced); Spiced Wine (127)

5 *A feast for about 30*

(most quantities should be doubled)

Bread, butter, and wine on the tables, as above

Hors d'œuvres: Fish in Jelly (27), Sausage Hedgehogs (29), Paris Pies (79)

Main dishes and side dishes: Gilded Chicken (65); Loin of Pork in Boar's Tail Sauce (74); Grilled Fish with Yellow Sauce (62); Rice with Shellfish (58); Roast Tongue (77); Giblets (102); Peas (20); Savory Rice (21, var. 1); Creamed Leeks (13); Turnips with Chestnuts (17); Green Pancakes (37)

Dessert: Strawberry Custard Tart (118); Pears in Wine Syrup (106); Fig Pudding (115); Sweet Fritters (119); Honey and Almond Candy (125); Wafers (126); Spiced Wine (127)

6 *A Chaucerian feast of dishes mentioned in Chaucer's poetry*

(increase quantities as necessary, depending on the number to be served)

On the table: Wastel (white) and Broun Breed; Boter; Whit and Reed Wyn; Mortreux (9 or 11)

Main dishes and side dishes: Pyk in Galantyne (55); Blankmanger (58 or 89); Stubbel Goos with Percely (67, var. 1 or 2); Chiknes with the Marybones (83);

Pyes (79 or 81) and/or Pastees (24 or 78); Potages of
Wortes (19), Pesene (20), and Lekes (13)
Dessert: Peres, Appels, and Grapes White and Rede; Chese;
Gyngebreed (122); Wafres (126); Ypocras (127)

In adjusting quantities, try to provide a taste of everything,
not a full helping, for every guest at a feast; thus, if you have
twenty guests and are serving Menu 4, you should have
twenty very small Brie tarts or two larger ones (each to be
cut into ten small slices); enough shrimps so that each diner
gets a tablespoon or two; and forty to sixty meatballs. One of
the most important considerations in planning any feast is
the tastes of those likely to sample the food. There should be
some familiar-looking dishes, as well as more exotic ones, not
a plethora of highly spiced stews. Following such principles is
more authentic as well as more pleasing to modern tastes.

For example, most menus should include some of the simple foods which will seem familiar to the most conservative
tastes, such as 20, 26, 42, 49, 64, 76, 114, and 118. Those
with an eye on costs should watch for such recipes as 10, 22,
28, 37, 45, 51, 80, 88, 102, 110, 112, and 122. Dishes with
special appeal for gourmets can be found everywhere but we
might draw special attention to 1, 39, 47, 54, 74, 91, 117,
and 121, as well as those mentioned on the first three menus
given above. Those who are watching for ways to use leftovers, including wilted flowers, will find some dishes which
demand such, including 11, 36, 52, 85, 87, 89, 95, 98, 100,
and 109.

Some may be shocked to hear that we usually serve sherry
before a feast, anachronistic as it may be when sack was,
apparently, not introduced into England until the sixteenth
century. As accompaniments to sherry, or simply set on the
table with the bread, butter, and table wine, we serve olives
and radishes, both of which are mentioned in some Continen-
tal menus as preceding the first course. We always serve a
table wine, or choice of table wines, with medieval food.
Those who prefer ale (or milk) will also be properly authentic, if not as aristocratic. Most commercially marketed mead

is too sweet to go with anything but a dessert course. And,
finally, for a proper feast we usually construct a proper subtlety. Any pastry cook, even a relatively inept one, can do
something in this line, although the more spectacular effects
can only be managed by those with plenty of experience at
producing elaborately decorated cakes.

The manner of service of a medieval meal does not really con-
cern us as much as the authenticity (and tastiness) of the
food. Those who yearn for real authenticity may use 'trenchers' instead of plates and deny their guests forks, which were
only used for serving in the middle ages. We find it more
comfortable to use our customary plates and forks. For a
feast we try to set up tables festively, with the white table-
cloths prescribed by medieval authorities and candles to provide illumination. We also see no reason to use medieval
kitchen tools and methods when better ones have replaced
the numerous servants of a large medieval household. Thus
we see no point in straining eggs when we can reach for a
whisk or egg beater, and we find a blender better than a mortar and pestle for most grinding. A mortar is especially useful,
however, for certain jobs such as pulverizing saffron or caraway seeds, both difficult chores – unless you have an electric
coffee grinder. Those who have no grinder and neither blender
nor mortar will have to try rubbing saffron (with some salt or
sugar, depending on the recipe) in a saucer with a spoon. In
any case, we have found that saffron is much easier to grind
if you dry it in a warm oven first.

Other substances which present special problems are galingale (or ginger root) and bread crumbs. We advise grating
galingale – if you have any – or ginger root with a nutmeg
grater or the fine edge of a grater one uses for lemon peel.
Bread crumbs, the ubiquitous thickening agent of so many
medieval sauces, were no doubt favoured because this was a
way to use up the leftover crusts and broken pieces of bread;
they are also practical because there is no need to make a
roux, as we usually do for a modern flour thickening. But in
no case should one try to use the packaged toasted bread-

crumbs available in boxes at the market. The result will be terribly gritty, and not really very thick. If the recipe calls for toast, use toast, broken into pieces; otherwise, the best breadcrumbs are made from fairly stale bread, ground in a blender or mortar, if possible. They can be rolled with a rolling pin, if necessary. In any case – whether the recipe calls for crumbs or soaked bread or toast – the smoothness of the sauce will be immeasurably better if the sauce is blended in a blender; failing that, blend the crumbs and part of the sauce very thoroughly (preferably in a mortar) before proceeding to the final step: and use a whisk, if possible.

Sometimes our recipes may appear to depart from the original version printed. This is because we have compared different versions of the same dish and when we found a more appealing feature from another source chose to incorporate it. However, we have avoided adding or subtracting anything unless at least one source justified the change. Substitutions are another question. There seems, for example, no good reason why a modern cook should not substitute cornstarch for rice flour if he has no rice flour and does not have a blender in which to pulverize rice grains; the effect will be the same. Nor are we fussy about the bread we serve, as long as it is crusty and reasonably chewy. Round loaves, or large buns, are the most authentic in appearance. We have experimented with barley flour and other grains much used in the middle ages, but it is easiest to rely on a local Portuguese bakery, or others which bake relatively coarse bread in round loaves, and to concentrate our efforts on other foods.

Spices remain a vexed question. We cannot even be sure that we know what some of the common spices were: the 'grains of paradise' sometimes called for is particularly baffling. Information in dictionaries seems to indicate cardamom, but this is questionable since both are occasionally called for in a single recipe. Cubebs and galingale are difficult to find today, but well worth trying if you can get any. It is hard to see why they ever went out of style, for both are delightfully aromatic. Those who cannot purchase them may

substitute pepper and cloves and ginger and cinnamon,
respectively: the result will not be all that different.

The evidence as to the nature of the various mixed spice 'powders' is even more confused. One recipe suggests ginger and white sugar as an alternative to 'powdor blanche' while another suggests ginger, cinnamon, and nutmeg – a very different mixture. Further, the latter is very close to the formula suggested elsewhere for 'powdor fort,' of ginger, cinnamon, and mace. Surely a *fort* powder must have been different from one that was *douce* (or *blanche*): some recipes call for a little of two different kinds. It may be thought that the *douce* varieties always contained sugar, but one must still be careful here, since some recipes call for sugar to be added as well as 'powdor douce.' Our general conclusion is that these mixtures must have varied with the individual cook or commercial supplier just as a modern 'curry powder' does – and that this is probably the most meaningful familiar parallel. Indian curries are often made with a particular blend made for the individual dish, and no two cooks are likely to use exactly the same blend, except that there are certain spices which are commonly found in a curry mixture – such as turmeric and chili peppers; another common Indian spice powder, garam masala, invariably excludes turmeric, whatever the proportions of other ingredients may be. The principle of making such powders is, clearly, to allow for the use of very small quantities of individual spices, mixed in a way that will suit the dish to be prepared, whether one buys the spices ready-mixed or grinds them oneself for a particular dish.

Thus, our advice to those making medieval dishes is to mix their own spices, either in a large batch from which a spoonful or two will be taken for this dish or that or in an individual mixture to compliment a particular dish. Mixed spices of the kind sold for apple pies may be used for many dishes, if one wishes. We have suggested particular combinations for each dish calling for unspecified 'powders,' but there is no reason why others should not vary our suggestions, as long as they aim at a stronger mixture for a fort powder as against a douce one. We think, for example, that it would be inadvisable to add pepper or cubebs to a douce powder, or sugar to a fort one. If a recipe calls for sugar, pepper, or another spice – such as ginger – as well as a powdor douce or powdor fort, this does not necessarily mean that there is none in the powder itself; it may simply mean that additional seasoning of the particular type is called for. Again, we draw the reader's attention to the fact that a curry recipe may call for curry powder *and* a particular spice which is represented to a lesser degree in the curry powder.

The sources from which we have drawn recipes are indicated by abbreviations at the end of each original version. These are all from fourteenth and fifteen century sources, although some of the scanty earlier collections have also been consulted, as well as a few slightly later in date. Roman sources, although still in circulation in manuscript in the middle ages, do not seem to have influenced later cooks, and have, thus, been ignored. The collections we found most useful are both fourteenth century: *The Ménagier de Paris* (MP) and *The Forme of Cury* (FC). Other abbreviations signify the following: AC: 'Ancient Cookery,' a two-part collection appended to FC in the printed editions; N: Napier's *A Noble Boke of Cookry*; LCC: *Liber Cure Cocorum;* HARL: ms Harleian, both 279 and 4016 (which one is indicated by number). Other mss are designated by their usual names. Recipes from various mss appear in a number of the books listed in the bibliography, page 161.

NOTES

1 See the bibliography for further information on this and all other sources cited, as well as generally informative works.
2 Readers who may be skeptical about whether we have done our scholarly homework are referred to the annotated bibliography and to C.B. Hieatt's forthcoming article ' "To boille the chiknes with the marybones": Hodge's Kitchen Revisited,' which goes into some of the matters touched on in a more thorough, and thoroughly annotated, version.

Soppes and Potages

In this section are all the dishes most likely to be considered soups today, as well as vegetables in broth which may be served either as soups or as accompaniments to meat. Thicker meat and fish pottages are listed in the sections on fish and stews; salads and fried or sautéed vegetables, in the section on entremets.

1 Tredure

Take Brede and grate it. Make a lyre of rawe ayren and do þer=to Safron and powdor douce and lye it up with gode broth; and make it as a Cawdel, and do þerto a lytel verious.

FC 15

Golden Soup

4 cups chicken, lamb, or pork broth
1 cup breadcrumbs
2 eggs, beaten
optional: 1/8 tsp each cardamon, coriander; pinch saffron
1/2 tsp salt (or to taste)
2 tbsp lemon juice

Bring the broth to a boil. Meanwhile, beat the breadcrumbs together with the eggs and spices. Off the heat, beat egg mixture into broth; return to very low heat for a few minutes, stirring constantly, to thicken a bit; do not allow mixture to boil. Stir in lemon juice.

2 Jowtes of Almand Mylke

Take erbes; boile hem, hewe hem, and grynde hem smale; and drawe hem up with water. Set hem on the fire and seeþ the jowtes with the mylke; and cast þeron sugar & salt, & serue it forth. FC 88

Green Almond Soup

ca 2 cups spinach (tightly packed down whole leaves –
   about 1/2 lb - raw; if you wish to use leftover cooked
   spinach, use about 1 cup, drained; less if the cooked
   spinach is chopped)
3-4 scallions, cut in pieces
2-3 sprigs parsley
6 cups water
1 1/2 tsp salt (or to taste)
1 tsp sugar
8 oz ground almonds or 4 oz almonds plus 1 tbsp cornstarch,
   dissolved in 2 tbsp cold water

Bring the water to a boil, adding salt; put in spinach and scallions and boil about 4 minutes; then add parsley, boil for a few more seconds, then remove from the heat. Drain, reserving the cooking water. Chop the vegetables very fine – or put in a blender with the almonds and a little of the cooking water and blend. Stir together greens, almonds, and all the reserved water, adding the sugar, in the saucepan, and return to the stove. Simmer together gently for about five minutes. Then stir in cornstarch dissolved in water, and simmer for a few more minutes before serving.

VARIATIONS
1 The soup may be chilled and served cold.
2 Watercress, sorrel, or other greens may be substituted for the spinach. A few leaves of fresh herbs from the garden, if you are lucky enough to have some, would be a welcome

addition, providing they are not added in such strength as to overwhelm the delicate flavour of the basic soup. (For this reason, dried herbs may be a bit dangerous.)

3 Sowpps Dorry

𝕹ym onyons and mynce hem smale and fry hem in oyl dolyf. 𝕹ym wyn and boyle yt wyth the onyouns; toste wyte bred and do yt in dischis, and god Almande mylk also, and do ther' abobe, and serbe yt forthe. AC.II.6

Other recipes for this soup, under the title of 'Sowp Dorry' or 'Soupes Dorroy,' etc, do not always include the onions: without them, it is simply a soup of almonds and wine indistinguishable from Cawdel of Almand Mylk (6); with them, it becomes a forerunner of the modern type of onion soup; but still quite different. Austin (p 127, 'Dorre') glosses as 'endored,' gilded; but such 'Sops' were not notably golden. Perhaps the etymology here is, rather, *du roi*, royal; wine was not a cheap ingredient.

Onion Soup

3 or 4 large onions, minced or thinly sliced
1/4 cup olive oil
1 bottle dry white wine (or use half wine and half water)
4 tbsp ground almonds
bread, sliced and toasted
salt to taste

Heat the oil in a large stew-pan and stir the onions in; let them cook over low heat, stirring occasionally, for 5-10 minutes. Meanwhile, soak the almonds in 1/2 cup of the wine plus 1/2 cup boiling water. Then add the rest of the wine to the onions; cover the pot and let simmer for 15 minutes; add

almond mixture and cook for a few more minutes. Salt to taste.

To serve in the true medieval style, place a slice of toasted bread in each serving bowl, and pour the soup over the toast. Such 'sops' give 'soup' its name.

4 𝕱enkel in 𝕾oppes

𝕮ake blades of 𝕱enkel; shrede hem not to smale, do hem to seeþ in water and oile and oynons mynced þerwith. 𝕯o þerto safron and salt and powdor douce. 𝕾erue it forth; take brede ptosted and lay the sewe onoward. FC 77

Fennel Soup

1 bunch fennel
2 onions, minced
4 cups water (more or less, depending on desired thickness
   and number to be served)
1/4 cup olive oil
optional: pinch saffron
1/8 tsp each ginger, pepper
1 tsp salt, or to taste

Cut the white part of the fennel into shreds – about one inch by 1/2 inch. (The green, feathery part of the fennel may be saved for salads or other uses – for example, see Spynoch Yfryed (40), and Salat (44).) Heat the oil in a heavy pot, and stir the onions and fennel in the oil over low heat until they are slightly wilted, but not browned. Add water, and seasonings, and bring to a boil. Simmer for about 20 minutes (or longer, if fennel does not seem tender). Place a slice of toasted bread in each bowl, and pour the soup over the toast.

VARIATION
Fennel cooked the same way, but with less water (1 cup is enough) may be served as a vegetable dish.

5 Blandissorpe

Take the ȝolkys of Eggs sodyn and temper it wyth mylk of a kow and do ther'to Comyn and Safron and flowr' of ris or wastel bred mynced and grynd in a morter and temper it up wyth the milk and mak it boyle and do ther'to wit of Egg' corbyn smale and tak fat chese and kerf ther'to wan the licour is boylyd and serve it forth. AC II.19

Even the etymology of this dish is somewhat confusing, since many of the recipes include (as this one does) saffron, so that it is hardly *'blanc.'* Most contain chicken meat rather than eggs and cheese, and are thickened with almonds and rice flour, using water rather than milk; many advise sweetening with sugar. Anyone who wishes to try such variants is welcome, but we rather prefer this one. If you wish to serve it as a thick sauce or side dish, use half the recommended amount of milk.

Soup of Milk, Eggs, and Cheese

6 eggs, hard boiled
3 cups milk
1/2 - 1 cup bread crumbs (depending on how finely ground)
   or 3 tbsp rice flour or cornstarch
1/4 tsp each cumin and saffron, ground (if you must grind the saffron yourself, do it in a mortar or saucer with the salt)
1/2 tsp salt
ca 3/4 cup soft or semi-soft cheese, cut into fairly small pieces

Beat together the egg yolks, milk, and all other ingredients except egg whites and cheese: a blender is useful for this. Cook, stirring constantly, in a pan over medium heat until thick. Then add the egg whites, minced, and cheese, and stir for a few minutes more before serving.

6 Cawdel of Almand Mylk

Take almands blanched and drawe hem up with wyne; do þerto powder of gynger and sugar, and color it with Safron. Boile it and serue it forth. FC 87

An otherwise similar recipe in the same collection calls for water rather than wine, omits saffron, and adds rice flour and salt. The Ménagier recommends making almond milk by mixing ground almonds with water in which onions have been cooked. All three sources have been drawn upon for the following recipe. If you wish to use this as a sauce, use somewhat less liquid (eg, 1 cup each white wine and water).

Almond Soup

2 oz (1/4 cup) ground almonds
2 tbsp rice flour or cornstarch
1 1/2 cups each white wine and water, preferably water in
   which onions have been parboiled
1/2 tsp salt
1/4 tsp each ginger, sugar
pinch ground saffron

Mix the almonds and rice flour or cornstarch with some of the wine (cold); add the ground spices and gradually stir in the rest of the liquids. Put over medium hot heat and bring to a boil, stirring. Simmer, stirring fairly frequently, for five to ten minutes, or until the soup seems thick enough. Serve hot.

VARIATION
For those who tire of the taste of saffron, try using rosé wine instead of white and omitting the saffron; it was not an invariable ingredient, as the notes above indicate, and rosé wine will give an equally interesting pastel colour — and slight flavour. (Remember, too, that for colour effects food colouring may be substituted for saffron.)

7 Oystrys in Bruette

Take an shele Oystrys, an kepe þe water þat cometh of hem, an strayne it, an put it in a potte, & Ale þer=to, an a lytil brede þer=to; put Gyngere, Canel, Pouder of Pepir þer=to, Safroun an Salt; an whan it is y=now al=moste, putte on þin Oystrys: loke þat þey ben wel y=wasshe for þe schullys: & þan serue forth. HARL 279.92

Oysters Stewed in Ale

8 oz oysters (use canned if you must, but fresh are much
  better)
12 oz ale
6 tbsp bread crumbs
1/8 tsp each ginger, cinnamon
1/4 tsp pepper
1/2 tsp salt
pinch of saffron (preferably ground)

Drain the liquid from shelled oysters (or the can, if using canned oysters) into a pan with the ale; add breadcrumbs and spices, and bring to a boil – carefully, as the ale is likely to foam over. Lower heat and stir for about five minutes, or until well blended and thickened to the consistency of a fairly thick soup. Then add oysters and stir a few minutes more. Serve hot. This amount will serve three generously, four more sparsely, as a first course; if you wish to serve as a main dish, allow this much for two.

8 Muscules in Broth

Take Muscules, And sith hem, and pike hem oute of the shell; And drawe the broth thorgh a strepnour into a faire vessell, And sette hit on the fire; And then take faire brede, and stepe hit with þe same broth, and draw hit thorgh a strepnour, And cast in-to a potte with þe sewe, and menge oynons, wyn, and pouder peper, and lete boyle; & cast there-to the Musculis and pouder ginger, and saffron, and salte; And then serue ye hit forthe. HARL 4016

Mussel Soup

1 qt fresh mussels, or at least 4 oz canned mussels (in brine)
1/4 cup breadcrumbs
2 onions, chopped, fried in a little oil or butter until soft but
   not brown
2 cups each white wine, mussel broth (add water to make up
   the necessary quantity, if using canned mussels)
1/4 tsp each pepper (white), ginger
pinch saffron

Scrub the mussels well and steam them in about 3 cups water, if using fresh mussels, for about 10 minutes. Remove from broth; allow to cool slightly and discard shells. Strain broth before proceeding. Moisten breadcrumbs with a little broth (brine from the can, if using canned mussels). While the crumbs steep for a few minutes, sauté onions. Blend crumb mixture in a blender or put through a strainer; then add to onions, together with wine, broth, and spices. Let simmer for at least 10 minutes before adding mussels; continue to heat just until mussels are heated through again.

VARIATIONS

Ale may be substituted for wine, or both omitted; a little vinegar may be added (preferably as a moistening for the crumbs), and/or other spices, such as cinnamon.

9 Whyte Mortrewes of Fysshe

Take codling, haddock or hake and lyveres with the rawnes and seep it well in water; pyke out þe bones, grynde smale the Fysshe, draw a lyour of almands & brede with the self broth; and do the Fysshe gronden þerto; and seep it and do þerto powdor fort, safron and salt, and make it stondyng.
FC 125

Other recipes for 'white' mortrews do not call for saffron, and we found it better to use other savory ingredients here.

Fish Soup or Pâté

1 lb cod or haddock, poached
2 cups water
1 cup white wine
1 slice onion
1 sprig parsley
1/4 cup each rice flour (or cornstarch), ground almonds
1 cup milk (or water, but in this case double the amount
   of almonds; cow's milk is cheaper than almond milk)
1 1/2 tsp salt (approximately)
1/4 tsp each white pepper, ginger
1/8 tsp nutmeg

Poach the fish in water and wine with the parsley, onion, and a little salt, for about ten minutes. Drain, straining broth. While fish is poaching, mix almonds and rice flour with milk and leave to steep. Put fish in blender (or use a mortar, followed by a strainer: blending is much easier) with enough of the strained broth to cover, and blend until smooth. Mix spices with a spoonful of water to completely dissolve. Then mix all ingredients together in a saucepan and simmer gently, for about five minutes, stirring. It should be a very thick soup. Taste for salt: underseasoning is inadvisable. It can be reheated later, but avoid boiling, as it may curdle.

To serve as a sort of paté rather than as soup, halve all liquid ingredients.

10 Roo Broth

Take the lire of the Deer oþer of the Roo; parboil it on smale peces. Seeþ it well, half in water and half in wyne. Take brede and bray it wiþ the self broth and drawe blode þer=to, and lat it seeth to=gedre with powdor fort of gynger oþer of cannell and macys, with a grete porcion of vinegar with Raysons of Corante. FC 14

This is a good way to use leftover bits of roast venison.

Venison Soup

ca 1 lb venison, cooked or parboiled, cut into small pieces
ca 1 1/2 cups each water, red wine
1/2 cup breadcrumbs (use wholewheat bread or rye – the
  darker the better)
1/4 tsp each ginger, cinnamon, mace
1 tsp salt
1/4 cup vinegar (preferably red wine vinegar)
1/4 cup currants
1 tsp Marmite, or other yeast-based gravy seasoning
  (in lieu of blood)

Cover the chopped venison with wine and water; simmer for about an hour. Steep the breadcrumbs in some of the broth (and the Marmite or other colouring), and stir into the pot, along with currants and seasonings. Simmer for about five minutes more, stirring occasionally, before serving.

11 Mortrews

Nym hennyn and porke and seth hem togedere. Nym the lyre of the hennyn and the porke and hakkyth smale and grynd hit al to dust, and wyte bred therwyth, and temper it wyth the selve broth and with heyryn, and colore it with saffron; and boyle it and disch it, and cast thereon powder of peper and of gyngynyr, and serve it forth. AC 5

Cream Soup of Pork and Chicken

ca 1 lb each (including bone) chicken and pork, or enough
  to yield around 2 cups cooked, chopped meat
2 slices bread (better if on the stale side)
2 eggs
large pinch saffron
1/4 tsp each ginger, white pepper
1 tsp salt (or more)

Cover the pork and chicken – or, if you are using leftover cooked meat, the bones and any odds and ends – with at least a quart of salted water. Wine (white) may be used for part of the cooking water, and a slice or two of onion adds to the flavour. Simmer for about an hour. Remove meat from broth, and discard all skin and bones. Strain broth and reserve. Cut the meat into small chunks and puree in a blender (or use a meat grinder or mortar: a blender is much the best, however) with bread, spices, eggs, and enough of the broth to cover amply. It should be very smooth. Stir into the rest of the broth, and cook over low heat, stirring constantly, until thick. If it curdles, blend again, or rub through a strainer. More water may be added if it is too thick, but it should be quite thick. Taste for salt: underseasoning is to be avoided.

VARIATIONS
1 Some recipes call for pork only.
2 A little ale (or beer) may be added at the moment when

the whole mixture comes to a boil; this helps to keep it from getting too hot and curdling. Try a half cup, if you wish. Sugar and/or cinnamon are sometimes added: 1 tsp sugar and 1/4 tsp cinnamon can be recommended.

See also Whyte Mortrewes of Fysshe (9): and note that with less liquid this can be served as a sort of paté.

12 Black Porray

Black porray is made with strips of spiced bacon. The por= ray should be picked over, washed, then cut up and blanched in boiling water, then fried in fat from the bacon slices; then you moisten it with boiling water—yet some say that if it is washed in cold water it is darker and more black—and you should set upon each bowl two slices of bacon. MP

The 'bowls' called for are probably servings for two though they may be individual bowls.

Greens braised with Bacon

2 lbs beet, dandelion, or other greens (such as spinach)
6-8 slices bacon

Pick over and wash the greens, then chop them and boil for three to five minutes in a large pot of boiling water; drain, and run cold water over them, then roll in paper towelling to dry as much as possible. Meanwhile, fry the bacon strips until brown and crisp, and set aside. Add the greens to the fat left in the frying pan and stir, over medium low heat, for several minutes, until well wilted and dark in colour. While the Ménagier calls for adding water at the moment before serving, this is not really necessary unless you wish to serve this as a soup. Serve with the bacon strips arranged over the top of the greens. If it is to be used as soup, add boiling water and crumble the bacon.

13 Blaunchyd Porray

Take thykke mylke of almondes dere
And leke hedes þou take with stalk in fere,
Þat is in peses þou stryke;
Put alle in pot, alye hit ilyke
With a lytel floure, and serve hit þenne
Wele soþun, in sale, before gode menne. LCC

Creamed Leeks

2 bunches of leeks, washed, trimmed, and sliced
2 tbsp ground almonds
2 tbsp flour (preferably instant-blending)
2 cups water, or 1 cup each water and milk
1 tsp salt

Mix the almonds and flour to a paste with a little of the water, and gradually beat in the rest of the water. (A blender is best, but it is not difficult to do by hand.) Bring to a boil, stirring, until the sauce is very thick. Add salt and sliced leeks and simmer for about ten minutes.

VARIATIONS
The Ménagier advises blanching (or parboiling, depending on the season: winter leeks, he says, are older and require full parboiling) the leeks; then adding them to some lightly fried onions until they wilt before putting them in white sauce to finish cooking. He recommends milk, except in Lent, when almond milk was necessary, and suggests bread as a thickening. On meat days, he adds, they may be cooked in a broth of pork or salted pork (ham, bacon) and served with bacon. If using any of these variations involving blanching or parboiling, cut the final cooking time in the sauce down to five minutes.

14 Caboches in Potage

Take Caboches and quarter hem and seeth hem in gode broth with Oynons y-mynced and the whyte of Lekes y-slit and corue smale, and do þer=to safron and salt, and force it with powdor douce. FC 4

After following these directions as exactly as possible, we concluded that the Ménagier of Paris is right in suggesting that it is a better idea to cut up cabbages before cooking them, rather than to cook them in such large pieces as quarters. Others may like it as well in the larger pieces, however.

Cabbage Stew

1 head cabbage, cut in quarters or shredded
2 onions, sliced thin or minced
2-3 leeks, washed and chopped
1/2 tsp salt (or less, if broth is well seasoned)
2 cups (approximately) meat broth or stock
1/8 tsp each cardamom and coriander (ground)
optional: 1 tsp sugar, pinch of saffron (scant)

Bring all ingredients to a boil and simmer for about 20 minutes (somewhat less if cabbage is shredded fine).

15 Gourdes in Potage

Take young Gowrds; pare hem and kerue hem on pecys; cast hem in gode broth, and do þer=to a gode party of Oynons mynced. Take Pork soden; grynd it and alye it þer=with and wiþ ȝolkes of ayren. Do þer=to safron and salt, and messe it forth with powder douce. FC 8

'Gourds' may mean gourds, squash, pumpkin, or even cucumbers. In this case, squash seems an appropriate choice, but pumpkin is perfectly feasible.

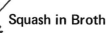

Squash in Broth

2 lbs squash or pumpkin, peeled, seeded, and cut into chunks
3-4 onions, minced
3 cups meat broth (approximately)
1/2-1 cup ground, cooked pork
2 egg yolks (or one whole egg), beaten
pinch saffron
salt to taste
1/8 tsp each cinnamon and ginger
1 tsp sugar

Boil the squash in the broth with the onions; stir in ground pork and seasonings when almost done. Take off the fire and beat in egg or egg yolks just before serving.

VARIATIONS
1 Parboil the squash in salted water for 20 minutes, or until soft; mash, and add beef or pork drippings rather than broth. Season with salt and saffron.
2 Prepare as in variation 1, but sprinkle the saffron over the cooked squash in threads as a decorative touch: the Ménagier says this is known as 'fringed with saffron.'

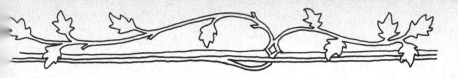

16 Rapes in Potage

Take rapus and make hem clene and waissh hem clene;
quare hem; parboile hem; take hem up, caste hem in a gode
broth and seeþ hem. Mynce Oynons and cast þer=to Safron
and Salt and messe it forth with powdor douce. In the wise
make of Pasturnakes and skyrwates. FC 5

Turnips in Broth

2 lbs white turnips, cut in quarters or chunks (after peeling)
2 cups meat broth
2 onions, minced
1/2 tsp salt
optional: pinch of saffron, and/or 1/8 tsp each cardamom
   and coriander; 1 tsp sugar

Parboil turnips in a pot of boiling, salted water for about 5
minutes; then drain, and put in a pan with onions, broth, and
seasonings, and simmer until tender (10-30 minutes, depending on the age and size of the turnips).

VARIATION
Cook parsnips, yellow turnips, or carrots the same way, or
try a mixture.

17 Tornep with Chestenne

Young, small turnips should be cooked in water without
wine for the first boiling. Then throw away the water
and cook slowly in water and wine, with chestnuts therein,
or, if one has no chestnuts, sage. MP

Even if one does have chestnuts, sage seems to improve the
dish.

Turnips with Chestnuts

2 lbs small white turnips, peeled (or use medium ones,
   peeled and quartered)
5 cups water
1 cup white wine
1/4 - 1/2 lb chestnuts, shelled (that is, as many as you
   have time and energy to shell), *and/or*
1/2 tsp dried sage, or a sprig of fresh sage (more if you are
   not using chestnuts)
salt

To shell chestnuts: one method is to pare off a strip of skin
from each chestnut (using a small, sharp knife), then drop
them, a few at a time, into boiling water. When they have
boiled a few minutes, remove from the water and peel off the
rest of the shell.

Parboil the turnips in 4 cups boiling, salted water for five
minutes. Drain and recover with remaining cup of water and
the wine; add shelled chestnuts and sage, as well as a little
more salt, and bring back to a boil. Lower the heat and simmer gently for about 30 minutes.

18 Funges

Take Funges and pare hem clene and dyce hem; take leke
and shred hym small and do hym to seeþ in gode broth. Color
it with safron and do þer-inne powdor fort. FC 10

Mushrooms

1 lb mushrooms, washed and sliced (not too thinly)
1 bunch leeks, washed and shredded
1-2 cups broth, preferably chicken

1/8 tsp each ginger, cardamom, allspice, white pepper
salt to taste
optional: pinch of saffron

Simmer vegetables and spices in the broth for 10-15 minutes. If you wish to serve this as a soup rather than as a vegetable dish, use more broth.

19 Buttered Wortes

Take al maner of good herbes that thou may gete, and do bi ham as is foresaid; putte hem on þe fire with faire water; put þere=to clarefied buttur a grete quantite. Whan thei ben boyled ynogh, salt hem; late none otemele come therein. Dise brede small in disshes, and powre on þe wortes, and serue hem forth. HARL 4016

The 'wortes' mentioned in the recipe occurring just before this in the ms include cabbage leaves, beet greens, borage, parsley, and leeks: in other words, use any combination of greens and vegetables of the onion family.

Buttered Greens

2-3 lbs mixed greens (spinach and parsley, if nothing else is in season)
2-3 leeks or onions
2 tbsp butter (or more)
4-6 slices bread, diced and lightly toasted

Blanch the greens and leeks or onions in a large pot of boiling, salted water for three or four minutes – no more. Drain, squeeze out excess water, and chop. Put in a pan with the butter and about 1/2 cup fresh water; stir, cover, and leave over very low heat for another five minutes. Salt to taste and serve, mixed with toasted bread cubes. (*more*)

Water may be decreased to 1/4 cup; on the other hand, if one desires to serve this as a soup, increase the water to 1 cup, or more – this is more probably the way it was served in the 15th century.

20 Grene Pesen

𝕿ake yonge grene pesen, and sethe hom with gode broth of beef, and take parsell, sage, saverap, and psope, and a lytel brede, and bray all this in a morter, and sume of the pesen therwyth, and tempur hit wyth the broth, and do hit in a pot to the other pesen, and let hit boyle togedur, and serve hit forth. ARUNDEL

Two closely related recipes advise only parsley and mint, or parsley and hyssop, so our feeling that these should be the preponderant herbs is strengthened.

Green Peas

3 lbs fresh green peas, shelled, or, if peas are out of season,
   2 packages of frozen peas
1 cup beef broth (or use chicken — it is just as good)
2 sprigs parsley
a few leaves of mint, or 1/2 tsp dried mint
1 or 2 sage leaves and a bit of savory
   (or 1/8 to 1/4 tsp each dried)
1 slice bread (slightly stale)

Boil the peas in broth until almost done (about 12 minutes). Grind herbs and bread in a mortar or blender with some of the broth; add about 1/2 cup of the cooked peas and continue to blend, adding more broth, until you have a smooth, fairly thick sauce. Drain the rest of the peas and reheat (gently) in this sauce.

21 Ryse of Flessh

Take Ryse and waisshe hem clene, and do hem in erthen pot with gode broth and lat hem seeþ wel. Afterward take Almand mylke and do þerto, and color it wiþ safron, and salt, and messe forth. FC 9

Rice in Meat Broth

1 cup raw rice
2 1/2 cups chicken or meat broth
2 tbsp ground almonds
1/2 tsp salt (or less, if broth is sufficiently salty)
pinch saffron

Put the rice in a pot with a well-fitting lid, and add 2 cups of the broth. Bring to a boil; cover and turn the heat down very low. Bring the rest of the broth to a boil separately; remove it from the heat and stir in almonds, saffron, and salt. Cover and let steep.

When the rice has been cooking for about 15 minutes, add the almond mixture, cover again, and let it continue to cook over very low heat for another five minutes, or until it has absorbed most of the moisture.

VARIATIONS
1 For Ris engoulé in the French style, rice should be washed in several waters, then cooked in rather more water than is advised above for about ten minutes, drained, and spread out in a large, flat pan and left in a warm place to dry out. (A low, or barely on, oven is fine.) Then add meat drippings and saffron, and cook for another five or ten minutes.
2 Ris engoulé to go with fish is made the same way except that almond milk (as above, but use water instead of broth) is used in place of drippings; the Ménagier advises a little sugar instead of saffron.

22 Frumenty

Nym clene Wete and bray it in a morter wel that the holys gon al of and sepþ yt til it breste and nym yt up, and lat it kele and nym fayre fresch broth and swete mylk of Almandys or swete mylk of kyne and temper yt al, and nym the yolkys of eyryn; boyle it a lityl and set yt adon and messe yt forthe wyth fat benyson and fresh moton. AC 1

Modern packagers of cracked wheat (or Bulgur, a popular variety) relieve us of the tedious preprocessing here. Egg yolks are not always called for, nor need one use two or more of the recommended liquids. Sweetened and/or with milk, the effect is like a modern breakfast porridge, but in broth this is an excellent accompaniment to meats.

Cracked Wheat

1 cup cracked wheat
3 cups meat or chicken stock or bouillion, or use half milk
optional: pinch of saffron, 1 or 2 egg yolks

Bring the stock to a boil and stir in the wheat (and saffron, if desired). Cover the pan and turn the heat very low; let the frumenty cook for about 45 minutes. It may be served then as it is, or you can remove it from the heat, stir in beaten egg yolk, then return to very low heat and stir for a few minutes before serving.

VARIATION
Barley was also used this way, and is excellent. Small pearl barley takes about the same time to cook, or just a little longer. If using barley, saffron is particularly desirable, and the egg added at the end a vast improvement.

Entremets

This section includes specialities suitable for serving as hors d'oeuvres and side dishes (although some of the latter may be found in the section on soups and pottages) as well as eggs and cold dishes. At a medieval feast such dishes were sometimes served as a first course, but usually appeared after the simpler roasts and pottages.

23 Tart de Bry

Take a Crust ynche depe in a trap. Take ȝolkes of Apren rawe and chese ruayn, & medle it & þe ȝolkes togyder; and do þerto powdor gynger, sugar, safron, and salt. Do it in a trap; bake it and serue it forth. FC 166

Brie Tart

pastry for one open tart shell or 2 dozen very small tarts
6 egg yolks (or 3 whole eggs)
5 oz soft, runny cheese, preferably Brie; rind pared off
1/4 tsp each ginger, salt
optional: 1/4 cup sugar (only if to be served as a dessert)
scant pinch saffron

Mash the cheese and beat in the eggs and seasonings; put in tart shell or shells and bake in a 375° oven for 15 to 20 minutes, or until *lightly* browned. Do not overcook, especially if they are to be reheated before serving (they should be served warm, if used as appetizers).

Ideally, mix this in a blender. If you have none, beat eggs well before adding mashed cheese, and beat until the whole mixture seems light, as well as thoroughly smooth. Do not overfill tart shells: about half-full is enough, as the mixture will puff during baking. This puffy effect may fall a bit when the tart is taken from the oven, but, if you are careful, there will still be a slightly rounded look to the top.

24 Mushroom Pasties

Mushrooms of one night are the best, if they are small, red inside, and closed at the top; and they should be peeled and then washed in hot water and parboiled, and if you wish to put them in a pasty add oil, cheese, and spice powder. MP

Perhaps it really was necessary to peel mushrooms and wash them in hot water in 14th century France, but we doubt that the kind of little button mushroom here described need be treated so today: a scrubbing in cold water should suffice. In making them into pasties, we prefer to use open tart shells, although medieval pasties were made like turnovers: one put the filling on top of a piece of rolled pastry, then doubled the pastry over and pinched the edges together. But this makes rather a lot of pastry in proportion to filling, particularly if you make them very small, as we do when serving a large number of people. We suspect medieval people also found all that pastry superfluous at a dinner with many courses, since the treatises on carving and serving at tables regularly advise the server to remove the top of the pasty and serve the contents.

Mushroom Pasties

One full recipe pastry (enough to make a two-crust pie),
   rolled and cut into pieces a little over twice the size of the
   desired pasties; *or* 12 small tart cases (made from your own
   pastry, or from the frozen food case at the supermarket)
3/4 lb small button mushrooms
1-2 oz cheese, grated: 1 oz each of cheddar and parmesan
   is excellent for this purpose
2 tbsp olive oil
1/2 tsp salt (approximately)
1/4 tsp ginger
1/8 tsp ground pepper

Wash mushrooms, and pare away the bottom of the stems, but leave whole. Parboil in salted water for 3-4 minutes. Drain, and mix with oil and seasonings; if you are using tart shells, rather than making a sort of turnover, reserve the cheese to sprinkle on top. Fill the tart shells or make turnovers; bake in a 425° oven for about 20 minutes, or until lightly browned.

VARIATION

A large open tart of mushrooms prepared in this way makes an excellent first-course dish for a dinner.

25 Tart in Ymbre Day

𝕿ake and parboile 𝕺ynons; presse out þe water & hewe hem smale; take brede & bray it in a mortar, and temper it up with 𝕬pren; do þerto butter, safron and salt, & raisons corans, & a litel sugar with powdor douce, and bake it in a trap, & serue it forth. FC 165

Tart for an Ember Day

2 large onions
1 tbsp melted butter
4 eggs
2 tbsp bread crumbs
pinch saffron
1/2 tsp salt
1/8 tsp sugar (plus, if you wish, a pinch of one or two mild
   spices, such as cardamom and mace)
ca 2 tbsp currants
unbaked pie shell

Parboil the onions for about five minutes; cool and chop (or

chop first, then parboil and strain: it is easier). Add butter to thoroughly drained onions. Mix remaining ingredients together in a bowl; add onions; pour into pie shell. Bake at 350° for 30 to 40 minutes, until the filling is set and the pastry lightly browned.

26 Creupce

Boil in water and wine and eat with vinegar. MP

Crayfish

Other shellfish may be treated the same way — lobster tails make a fine substitute for crayfish, though the frozen ones are apt to be a bit tough. Crayfish, like shrimp, should be cleaned after cooking, to remove the intestinal tract. Medieval authorities counsel one to remove the flesh of crayfish or crab from the shell and cut the meat into strips; legs, however, can be served in the shell, with the shell cracked. Shrimps were served shelled. John Russell counsels,

Shrympes welle pyked, þe scales away ye cast,
Round abowt a sawcer ley ye þem in hast;
Þe vinegre in þe same sawcer, þat youre lord may attast,
Þan with þe said fische he may fede hym & of þem
make no wast.

27 Gele of Fyssh

Take Tenches, pykes, eelps, turbot, and plays; kerue hem to pecys. Scalde hem & waische hem clene. Drye hem with a cloth and do hem in a pane; do þerto half vynegar & half wyne & seeth it wel; & take the Fysche and pike it clene; cole the broth thurgh a cloth into an erthen pane. Do þerto

powdor of pepper and safron ynowþ. Lat it seeþ and skym it wel whan it is ysode; dof þe grees clene; cowche fisshe on chargeors & cole the sewe thorow a cloth onoward, & serue it forth. FC 101

This particular recipe does not seem to be a cold, jellied dish, and those who so wish may serve it hot. However, comparison with similar recipes, which are explicit on this point, makes it clear that such dishes often were jelled: a version we prefer. The jelling was effected by the concentration of fish: other recipes tell us to add fish skins, etc, if the liquid will not 'catch.' Modern cooks will find it easier and safer to add powdered geletine. Later recipes often allowed for water, as well as wine and vinegar, in the cooking broth; a combination of these, with higher proportions of the wine and vinegar than is apt to be found in a more modern recipe, produced a highly satisfactory flavour.

The most attractive way to present this dish is to use one whole fish and cut other, smaller fish into slices (through the spine). This will produce a handsome dish if you have an oval dish a little longer than the whole fish in which to arrange the effect. Another consideration is that the jelly should cover the fish: so measure the content of your serving dish and calculate the amount of liquid needed to exactly cover the fish before you start, adjusting the quantities accordingly.

Fish in Jelly

1 whole fish, ca 1 1/2 to 2 lbs (pike, bass, trout, or pickerel are suitable; or try flounder, plaice, or a flatter fish, if you can get one with the skin on)
ca 1 lb smaller fish (eel is particularly suitable) cut into slices about an inch thick
2 cups each water, vinegar, and white wine – or more, if needed to cover fish while it poaches: if liquid must be increased, use the same proportions

1/4 tsp salt (or more, in proportion to liquid)
1/8 tsp ground white pepper
pinch saffron
1 envelope unflavoured gelatine, soaked in 1/4 cup cold water

Bring cooking broth (water, wine, and vinegar) to a boil; salt and turn down the heat. Poach the fish *gently* in this broth for 15-20 minutes, adding the cut-up pieces of fish after the whole fish has been cooking for 5-10 minutes. Be sure to remove the fish before it shows signs of beginning to fall apart. Put it aside and allow to cool. Add the pepper and saffron to the cooking broth and leave it to steep while the fish cools.

Skin the fish carefully and arrange in the serving dish, with the smaller pieces around the whole fish. Soak the gelatine, and let it stand while you strain the broth and bring 2 1/2 cups of the strained broth to a boil. (If you need to increase the amount of broth by more than a half cup, you will have to increase the amount of gelatine also.) Off the heat, stir the measured, hot broth into the soaked gelatine, stirring until well dissolved. Pour this over the fish in its dish.

If you wish to decorate the dish further, use sprigs of parsley and/or slivered blanched almonds. When cool, put in refrigerator or other cool place to chill until well set.

28 Pommeaulx

Take fayre buttys of Vele and hewe hem, and grynd hem in a morter, and wyth þe ȝolkes of eyroun, and with þe whyte of eyroun; and caste þer-to powder Peppr, Canel, Gyngere, Clowys powþer, and datys y-mynced, Safroun, and raysonys of Coraunce, and sethe in a panne wyth fayre water, and let it boyle; þan wete þin handys in Raw eyroun, þan take it and rolle it in þin handys, smaller or gretter, as þow wolt haue it, an caste it in-to boyling water, an let boyle y-now; þan putte it on a Spete round and let hem rosty; þen take flowre an ȝolkes of eyroun, an þe whyte, and draw hem þorwe a straynowre, an caste þer-to pouder Gyngere, an make

þin bature grene with þe Ius of Percely, or Malwys, in tyme of ȝere Whete, an caste on þe pommys as þey turne a-boute, and serve forth. HARL 279.46

Comparison with similar recipes indicates that, as usual, considerable leeway is available to the cook in making such meatballs. Sometimes the meat was boiled before it was chopped up; sometimes balls were poached in a sauce rather than grilled: the sauce specified for poaching Pumpes is a white sauce made with almond milk and rice flour, and seasoned with mace. We prefer our Pommeaulx small (no more than two inches in diameter). A composite recipe:

Meat Balls

2 lbs ground meat (veal, pork, lamb, beef, or a combination)
2 eggs, slightly beaten
1 tsp salt
1/2 tsp each ground ginger and mace
1/4 tsp each ground cardamom and cinnamon
1/8 tsp ground cloves
finely minced parsley, and/or flour, ginger

Moisten meat and seasoning with beaten eggs, mixing thoroughly. Shape into balls. Parboil in salted water: ca 10 minutes for pork, but 5 minutes is enough for small balls of other meats. Put on skewers and grill, turning regularly. When almost done, sprinkle with flour mixed with a little ginger and/ or finely minced parsley, or just the parsley. Do not overcook after adding one of these finishes, especially if meatballs are to be reheated before serving.

VARIATIONS

1 Pumpes: use ground, cooked pork, with chopped currants, as a base; season with ground cloves and mace, and, instead of eggs, moisten with a mixture of ground almonds and water or stock (ca 1/4 cup water, boiling, to a tbsp of almonds,

allowed to steep for at least 15 minutes before using) and add 1-2 tbsp rice flour or cornstarch to make it thick and cohesive enough to boil without losing shape.

2 Pome dorres: use ground raw pork and whites of eggs rather than whole eggs; gild by brushing on, in the last stages of cooking, a mixture of almond milk (made with ground almonds and water or broth) with flour, sugar, and eggs, with or without something to make the glaze green (parsley juice, for example – or green food colouring). *Or*: use raw ground beef and egg white, adding currents and seasoning with pepper. This variation advises simply gilding with egg yolk (cf Chicke Endored, 65).

29 Urchouns

Take Piggis mawys & skalde hem wel; take groundyn Porke & knede it with Spicerye, with pouder Gyngere, and Salt and Sugre; do it on the mawe, but fille it nowt to fulle, þen sewe hem with a fayre þrede and putte hem in a Spete as men don piggys. Take blaunchid Almoundys & kerf hem long, smal, and scharpe, & frye hem in grece & sugre. Take a litel prycke & pryckke þe yrchons. An putte in þe holes the Almundys, every hole half, & leche fro oþer. Ley hem þen to the fyre; when they ben rostid, dore hem, sum wyth Whete Flowre & mylke of Almaundys, sum grene, sum blake wiþ Blode, and lat hem nowt browne to moche; & serue forth. HARL 279.20

This recipe calls for a giant sausage made of a pig's stomach stuffed with ground spiced pork (a sort of sausage meat) and decorated with slivered almonds to form the spines of the 'hedgehogs.' Partly because giant sausages are difficult for the amateur medieval cook to make and partly because the larger the sausage the more difficult it is to get the pork cooked thoroughly, we prefer to make these much smaller and serve them as appetizers. The final coloured decoration is not essential, but can easily be accomplished with the use of some

food colouring, mixed with thin flour paste, if the cook so desires.

Sausage Hedgehogs

2 lbs ground pork
2 tsp ginger
1 tsp each salt, sugar
2 oz almonds, blanched and slivered (not sliced)

Mix pork and spices and form into balls about 1 1/2 to 2 inches in diameter; then elongate the balls a little, into ovals shaped like large walnuts (and about the same size). It is not absolutely necessary to fry the slivered almonds before using them – and may be dangerous, since they have a tendency to get overdone and turn black in the later baking – but a few minutes of sautéing over low heat, with a sprinkling of sugar, may help to make them less brittle and thus easier to handle. Insert them into the 'hedgehogs' in a pattern suggesting quills – you will need at least eight small spines for each ball to achieve the proper effect. Bake on a cookie sheet in a 350° oven for about 30 minutes, or until a good shade of medium brown. To reheat (if necessary), put in a hot oven for only a few minutes. Drain on paper towelling for a minute or two before serving.

If you wish to add the coloured decoration suggested above, this should be done just before the last few minutes of cooking; if done earlier, it will, of course, discolour.

VARIATION
Hedgehogs may be made out of ready-made sausage meat, but the flavour will, of course, be more ordinary.

Note: 'Hedgehogs can be made out of mutton tripe, and it is a great expense and a great labour and little honour and profit.' (MP)

30 Charlet

𝕿𝖆𝖐𝖊 𝕻𝖔𝖗𝖐 𝖆𝖓𝖉 𝖘𝖊𝖊𝖕 𝖎𝖙 𝖜𝖊𝖑. 𝕳𝖊𝖜𝖊 𝖎𝖙 𝖘𝖒𝖆𝖑𝖊; 𝖈𝖆𝖘𝖙 𝖎𝖙 𝖎𝖓 𝖆 𝖕𝖆𝖓𝖓𝖊. 𝕭𝖗𝖊𝖐𝖊 𝖆𝖞𝖗𝖊𝖓 𝖆𝖓𝖉 𝖉𝖔 𝖕𝖊𝖗𝖙𝖔, 𝖆𝖓𝖉 𝖘𝖙𝖜𝖞𝖓𝖌 𝖎𝖙 𝖜𝖊𝖑 𝖙𝖔𝖌𝖞𝖉𝖊𝖗. 𝕯𝖔 𝖕𝖊𝖗𝖙𝖔 𝕮𝖔𝖜𝖊 𝖒𝖞𝖑𝖐𝖊 𝖆𝖓𝖉 𝕾𝖆𝖋𝖗𝖔𝖓, 𝖆𝖓𝖉 𝖇𝖔𝖎𝖑𝖊 𝖎𝖙 𝖙𝖔𝖌𝖞𝖉𝖊𝖗. 𝕾𝖆𝖑𝖙 𝖎𝖙 & 𝖒𝖊𝖘𝖘𝖊 𝖎𝖙 𝖋𝖔𝖗𝖙𝖍. FC 39

Pork Hash with Egg

ca 2 cups cooked pork, minced or coarsely ground
4 eggs, lightly beaten
1 cup milk
1/2 tsp salt, or to taste
small pinch saffron

Put the pork in a saucepan or skillet; mix in eggs beaten with milk and seasonings. Cook, stirring, over low to medium heat until the sauce is quite well set. If it is cooked too quickly the eggs will curdle a little, but since the effect is simply scrambling, this is not a disaster.

VARIATIONS
1 Veal may be used in place of pork.
2 A pinch of sage may be added; and/or stir in a little ale or beer at the moment when the mixture reaches the boiling point: this helps to prevent separation of the sauce.
3 For a Charlet y-forced (in sauce), make a separate sauce of milk or almond milk (ground almonds steeped in broth – or water or milk) and thicken with egg yolks. This should be seasoned with some or all of (but be sparing): ginger, mace, clove, galingale, sugar, saffron, cinnamon. Some recipes also call for the addition of wine. To serve, put the Charlet on a serving platter and pour the sauce over it.

31 Sawge Y-farced

Take Sawge; grynde it and temper it up with ayren; a[nd] sawcystes & kerf hym to gobettes and cast it in a posynet; and do þerwiþ grece & frye it. Whan it is fryed ynow3, cast þerto sawge with ayren — make it not to harde; cast þerto powdour douce, messe it forth. FC 160

Sausage with Sage-Flavoured Scrambled Egg Sauce

1 1/2 lb smoked sausage (comparison with the recipe for
    sausage given by the Ménagier suggests that medieval
    sausages were smoked)
1/2-1 tsp chopped sage, depending on freshness and strength
8 eggs, beaten
ca 1/4 tsp each sugar, ginger
ca 1/8 tsp cinnamon
1 tbsp lard or other cooking fat

Slice the sausage into chunks. Brown it in a frying pan in the fat; when it is well cooked, drain off excess fat (leaving no more than 2 tbsp), stir in eggs and sage, and continue to stir over low heat until eggs are set but still soft. Add spices and serve at once.

32 Erbolat

Take parsel, mynts, sauery, & sauge, tansey, veruayn,
clarry, rew, ditayn, fenel, southrenwode; hewe hem & grinde
hem smale; medle hem up with Ayren; do butter in a trap;
& do þe fars þerto; & bake it & messe it forth. FC 172

Herb Custard

a small handful of whatever greens and herbs you can get:
   preferably including parsley, mint, sage, savory, and fennel
   leaves; in lieu of some of the less common ones, use a bit
   of spinach or other leafy greens – and in much larger proportion than the more strongly flavoured herbs
6 eggs, well beaten
1/2 tsp salt (or to taste)
1-2 tablespoons butter

Chop the greens and herbs as finely as possible and beat into
the eggs; a blender will do it all at once, of course. Add salt.
Melt the butter and pour it into a baking dish; tilt the dish
around to coat it well with the butter before adding the egg
and herb mixture. Bake in a 325° oven for 15 to 20 minutes,
or until well set but not dried out. (Test by inserting a knife
blade or toothpick.)

VARIATION

The Ménagier advises cooking this mixture in a frying pan as
an omelet, sprinkling grated cheese on the top when the eggs
are beginning to set on the bottom (he cautions that the
cheese should not be mixed in because it will make the eggs
stick to the bottom of the pan). His recipe also adds a bit of
ginger, and specifies as quantities to mix with 16 eggs (for
two very large omelets): half a leaf of rue, 2 leaves of dittany,
four each of smallage (wild celery), tansey, mint, and sage; a
little more in graduated steps upward, of marjoram, fennel,
and parsley; and two large handfuls of such greens as beet

greens, violet leaves, spinach, lettuces, and clary (a member of the mint family, but not so strongly flavoured). These proportions can, at least, serve as a guide.

33 Eggys Ryal

Cook onions, parboiling them for a long time ... then fry them; afterwards empty the pan in which you have fried eggs so that nothing is left in it, and in it put water and onions and a quarter part of vinegar, so that the vinegar is a quarter of the whole quantity; and boil it and pour it over the eggs. MP

The name for this dish is borrowed from an early 15th century menu; no corresponding recipe seems to exist in English sources. But this is interesting enough to rate a very special name. Lovers of Eggs Benedict are urged to try this simpler, less rich, but subtly tangy dish.

Royal Eggs

6 eggs
2 medium large onions, peeled
1/3 cup olive oil
3 tbsp vinegar
1/2 tsp salt

Cover the whole onions with salted water to cover and parboil for ca 10 minutes; then drain, reserving the onion water. Part of it will be used in the sauce; the rest can be used for recipes in which an onion-flavoured water is appropriate, such as Cawdel of Almond Mylk (6). When the onions have cooled a little, slice them. Heat olive oil in a large frying pan and fry onions until wilted and slightly golden. Remove and

reserve; add eggs and fry them in the same oil. Remove eggs to a serving platter when done. Then put onions back in the pan with 1/3 cup of the water in which they were cooked, vinegar, and salt. Boil for a few minutes, then pour over the eggs and serve at once.

34 Pochee

Take Apren and breke hem in scalding hoot water; and whan þei bene sode ynowh, take hem up and take зolkes of apren and rawe mylke and swyng hem togydre; and do þerto powdor gynger, safron, and salt; set it ouer þe fire, and lat it not boile, and take apren isode & cast þe sew onoward; & serue it forth. FC 90

Poached Eggs with Cream Sauce

for 6-8 poached eggs
3 egg yolks or 1 whole egg plus 1 yolk
1 1/2 cups milk
optional: pinch ground saffron
1/8 tsp ginger
1/4 tsp salt

Poach the eggs in water just below the boiling point; when they are done, remove to serving platter or plates. Meanwhile, beat the egg yolks or remaining eggs; heat milk to scalding, and gradually beat into the egg mixture. Put this sauce in a pan over very low heat, stirring continually, until thick; do not allow to boil. Season and pour over the poached eggs.

35 A Disshe mete for Somere

Take garbage of capons, and of hennes, and of chekyns, and of dowes, and make hom clene, and sethe hem, and cut hom smal, and take parsel and hew hit smal, and dresse hit in platers, and poure vynegur thereon, and caste thereon pouder of gynger, and of canel, and serve hit forthe colde at nyght.

ARUNDEL

Cold Chicken Livers

1 lb chicken livers
1 cup (ca) chicken stock *or* a mixture of water and red wine
1/2 tsp salt
2-3 tbsp minced fresh parsley
2 tbsp wine vinegar
1/8 tsp each cinnamon and ginger, mixed with 1/4 tsp salt

Put the livers and the 1/2 tsp salt in a small saucepan and cover with stock or wine and water; bring to a boil and simmer for about 5 minutes. Drain livers and chill. Just before serving, mix with parsley and vinegar and sprinkle the spice powder over the top. This can be served with toothpicks as an hors d'œuvre, or on pieces of toast or bread as a canape.

36 Pigge in Sauge

Take a pigge; Draw him, smyte of his hede, kutte him in iiij. quarters, boyle him til he be ynow; take him uppe, and lete cole; smyte him in peces; take an hondefull or ij of Sauge; wassh hit, grynde it in a morter with hard yolkes of egges; then drawe hit uppe with goode vinegre, but make hit not to thyn; then seson hit with powder of Peper, ginger, and salt; then cowche thi pigge in disshes, and caste þe sirippe þer-uppon, and serue it forthe. HARL 4016

That this is a cold dish is evident in the French version, Froide Sauge.

Cold Pork with Sage Sauce

Cold, sliced roast (or boiled) pork, to serve 4-6 people:
about 1 1/2 lbs. (We have used the leftovers from a
previously cooked larger roast.)
2 tbsp dried sage or about 12 fresh leaves, chopped
1-2 tsp finely chopped parsley
(may be omitted with fresh sage)
4 hardboiled eggs
1/4 cup vinegar (approximately)
1/2 tsp salt
1/8 tsp each pepper, ginger

Separate yolks and whites of boiled eggs. Mash the yolks with the sage and parsley – preferably in a morter; a blender may be used, but if so vinegar should be added at this point. Chop whites as finely as possible separately. Add to yolk and herb mixture with vinegar (if not already added) and other seasonings. If mixture seems too thick, add a little more vinegar.

Arrange the sliced pork on a suitable platter or dish for serving, and pour the sauce over it. (It is best to do this at the last minute: this sauce is not meant to be a marinade.)

VARIATIONS
Some similar recipes specify additional ingredients and/or alternate meats; for example:
1 other spices – galingale, cloves, cinnamon, cardamom – may be used;
2 a thickening of breadcrumbs steeped in broth, wine, or vinegar – but in this case use fewer eggs in the sauce and put a decorative garnish of hardboiled eggs around the dish.
3 Chicken or fish (either, skinned) may be used instead of pork.

37 Tansy Cake

Breke egges in basspn and swpng hem sone,
Do powder of peper her to anone;
Pen grpnde tansp, ho iuse owte wrpnge,
To blpnde with ho egges with owte lespnge.
In pan or skelet hou shalt hit frpe,
In butter wele skpmmet wpturlp,
Or white grece hou make take her to,
Geder hit on a cake, henne hase hou do,
With platere of tre, and frpe hit browne.
On brode leches serve hit hou schalle,
With fraunche mele or oher metes with alle. LCC

Other recipes for tansy cakes seem to call for smaller cakes, thickened with breadcrumbs (and in a later period, flour), with spice added. Since small pancakes seem more attractive than a cut-up green omelet, we have adapted the recipe to follow other examples. Tansy is a bitter herb not much in use today, but other recipes indicate almost any green, leafy vegetable may be substituted – one specifies 'spinage,' which satisfies us, though tansy is a sharper, more bitter herb. Others may wish to try more exotic leaves.

Green Pancakes

1 cup blanched spinach (parboiled for 4-5 minutes)
1 cup light cream
3 eggs
1 cup fine breadcrumbs
1/8 tsp each ground nutmeg and ginger
butter for frying

Drain spinach and squeeze out excess water with your hand. If you have a blender, put in blender with all other ingredients and blend until smooth; otherwise, chop spinach as finely as possible, then beat together with eggs, cream, and

seasonings. If batter is too thick, thin with cream or milk; cook as small, thin pancakes.

As with other such crepes, you may put the cakes aside when they are done, refrigerate, and reheat later in a medium oven.

38 Frytor of Erbes

Take gode erbys; grynde hem and medle hem with flour and water, a lytel zest and salt, and frye hem in oyle; and ete hem with clere hony. FC 151

This makes a pleasant and unusual accompaniment for roast meats – but for this purpose the honey can well be omitted.

Herb Fritters

1 package yeast
1 1/4 cups water (lukewarm)
1 cup flour
3-4 tbsp mixed green herbs: eg, 3 tbsp fresh parsley plus
    1/2 tsp each dried thyme, savory, and marjoram
1/4 tsp salt

Dissolve yeast in 1/4 cup lukewarm water, stirring. Then mix in flour, rest of water, and finely chopped herbs. Cover (a bit of plastic wrap is fine) and set in a warm place (for example, the back of the stove, presuming you are cooking something else in the oven or on the front burners at the time) for about an hour. Then drop by spoonfuls into fairly hot oil and fry, turning over once if you are not using deep fat.

39 Frytours of Pasternakes

Take skyrwats and pasternaks and apples, & parboile hem; make a bator of floer and ayren; cast þerto ale, safron & salt; wete hem in þe bator and frye hem in oile or in grece; do þerto Almand Mylk, & serue it forth. FC 149

This is a savory, rather than a sweet, fritter, and we assume that one need not use more than one of the root vegetables suggested, let alone combine apples and root vegetables.

Parsnip Fritters

2-4 parsnips (depending on size), peeled and sliced
1 package yeast (optional), dissolved in 1/4 cup lukewarm
  ale or beer
2/3 cup lukewarm ale or beer (in addition to any used to
  dissolve yeast)
1 cup flour
2 beaten eggs
1/2 tsp salt
optional: pinch of saffron (for colour);
  4 tbsp ground almonds (for sauce)

If using yeast, start by dissolving the yeast; let it sit a few minutes, then stir in the rest of the ale or beer, flour, salt, and egg. Put in a warm place (such as the back of the stove, if you are using the front burners) to rise for about an hour. Meanwhile, parboil the parsnips in salted water for about 20 minutes; drain, reserving cooking water if a sauce is desired. If you have not made a yeast batter, mix the rest of the ingredients for batter at this point.

Stir the parsnip slices into the bowl of batter, so as to coat each piece. Fry the fritters in deep fat, or in a little oil in a frying pan, turning them over as they brown; drain on paper. If a sauce is desired, beat some of the water in which the parsnips were cooked into the ground almonds until the desired

consistency is reached; season this with salt to taste, and add ground saffron if you wish to colour it.

VARIATION

Turnips, carrots, or apples may be substituted for the parsnips. Carrots should be parboiled for only 5 minutes, however, and apples not at all.

40 Spynoch Yfryed

𝕿ake 𝕾pynoches; parboile hem in sebyng water. 𝕿ake hem up and presse out þe water and hewe in two. 𝕵rye hem in oile clene, & do þer=to powder & serue forth. FC 180

This recipe for spinach is almost exactly what a contemporary French cook would specify.

Braised Spinach

2 lbs fresh spinach, washed and with excess stems and
  withered leaves removed
salted water for parboiling
ca 2-3 tbsp oil (preferably olive oil)
1/4 tsp salt
pinch each ginger, allspice

Parboil the spinach in a large pot of water for about 4 minutes; drain, press out excess water with your hands, and chop the spinach; put in a saucepan or small casserole with oil and seasonings. Stir, and leave to cook over very low heat for another 15 minutes or so; or put covered casserole in a low oven for about 20 minutes.

VARIATIONS

1 Beet or other greens may be cooked in the same way.
2 Add parsley and/or fennel with a little chicken or beef broth, instead of oil. *(more)*

3 Cook in water with a tbsp of vinegar added; then, instead of broth or oil, use 2 tbsp butter, and, if you wish, some grated cheese: the Ménagier suggests this.

41 Peascoddes

In cooking new peas to be eaten in the pod, one should put them in lard, on a meat-day; and on a fish day, when they have been cooked, pour away the water and put under them salted butter to melt, and then stir. MP

Jane Grigson informs us that in China street vendors sell peas cooked in their pods. The pod is picked up in the fingers, the peas which have been steamed inside sucked out, and the edible part of the pod then eaten, rather as we eat artichokes. The remaining fibrous part of the pod is discarded.

Peascoddes

2 lbs young peas in the pod
2 tbsp butter
water, salt

Leave the pods whole. If the stem end is cut off, the pods break open during cooking. Boil the peapods for 10-15 minutes, depending on size. Drain. Put into serving bowl or individual bowls, add butter, stir to coat.

Clearly, the original recipe calls for cooking the peapods with lard rather than butter whenever the fasts of the church

permit this; possibly, it is also meant that the cooking fluid on a 'meat day' ought to be meat (or chicken) broth. However, most modern diners ought to be content with the 'fasting' version of the dish.

42 𝔐𝔦𝔫𝔠𝔢𝔰

𝔏𝔦𝔱𝔱𝔩𝔢 𝔠𝔞𝔟𝔟𝔞𝔤𝔢𝔰 𝔠𝔞𝔩𝔩𝔢𝔡 𝔪𝔦𝔫𝔠𝔢𝔰 𝔞𝔯𝔢 𝔢𝔞𝔱𝔢𝔫 𝔴𝔦𝔱𝔥 𝔯𝔞𝔴 𝔥𝔢𝔯𝔟𝔰 𝔦𝔫 𝔳𝔦𝔫𝔢𝔤𝔞𝔯; 𝔞𝔫𝔡 𝔦𝔣 𝔬𝔫𝔢 𝔥𝔞𝔰 𝔭𝔩𝔢𝔫𝔱𝔶, 𝔱𝔥𝔢𝔶 𝔞𝔯𝔢 𝔤𝔬𝔬𝔡 𝔰𝔥𝔢𝔩𝔩𝔢𝔡, 𝔴𝔞𝔰𝔥𝔢𝔡 𝔦𝔫 𝔥𝔬𝔱 𝔴𝔞𝔱𝔢𝔯, 𝔞𝔫𝔡 𝔠𝔬𝔬𝔨𝔢𝔡 𝔴𝔥𝔬𝔩𝔢 𝔴𝔦𝔱𝔥 𝔞 𝔩𝔦𝔱𝔱𝔩𝔢 𝔴𝔞𝔱𝔢𝔯; 𝔞𝔫𝔡 𝔴𝔥𝔢𝔫 𝔱𝔥𝔢𝔶 𝔞𝔯𝔢 𝔠𝔬𝔬𝔨𝔢𝔡, 𝔞𝔡𝔡 𝔰𝔬𝔪𝔢 𝔰𝔞𝔩𝔱 𝔞𝔫𝔡 𝔬𝔦𝔩 𝔞𝔫𝔡 𝔰𝔢𝔯𝔳𝔢 𝔱𝔥𝔦𝔠𝔨, 𝔴𝔦𝔱𝔥𝔬𝔲𝔱 𝔴𝔞𝔱𝔢𝔯, 𝔞𝔫𝔡 𝔭𝔲𝔱 𝔬𝔩𝔦𝔳𝔢 𝔬𝔦𝔩 𝔬𝔫 𝔱𝔥𝔢𝔪 𝔦𝔫 𝔏𝔢𝔫𝔱. MP

The last part of these directions suggest that something other than oil was normally used outside of Lent: presumably, then, butter or meat fats may be used in place of oil as a dressing. A very simple recipe.

Brussels Sprouts

2 lbs Brussel sprouts – or according to number to be served
water, oil, salt

Trim and wash the sprouts and cook them in a pot of salted water until tender (10 minutes, approximately). Drain and add about 1 tbsp oil per pound of sprouts; salt to taste. Serve at once. Substitute butter or other cooking fat for the oil if you wish, but the taste of real olive oil will give the vegetable a slightly different character from the familiar plain buttered sprouts.

43 Benes Yfryed

Take benes and seeþ hem almost til þey bersten; take and
wryng out þis water clene; do þerto Oynons ysode and
ymynced, and garlec þerwith; frye hem in oile oþer in grece,
 & do þerto powdor douce, & serue it forth. FC 181

Fried Beans

1 lb fresh shell beans, shelled and boiled until tender,
  or a large can of boiled, shelled beans, drained
2 onions
2 cloves of garlic, minced or crushed
oil or other cooking fat

If you are cooking fresh beans, parboil the onions with the
beans for a few minutes, then remove them and allow them
to cool before you proceed to mince them. Or, simply mince
the onions and proceed without the step of parboiling them,
if you wish. In any case, drain the beans thoroughly and mix
with chopped onion and garlic; then sautee the vegetables,
stirring to keep them from sticking or over-browning, for
about five minutes.

44 Salat

Take parsel, sawge, garlec, chibollas, onyons, leeks, bor=
age, myntes, porrectes, fenel, and ton tressis, rew, rose=
marye, purslyne. Lave, and waishe hem clene; pike hem,
pluk hem small with þyn honde and myng hem wel with
rawe oile. Lay on vynegar and salt, and serve it forth.

FC 76

The greens and herbs called for in this recipe were un-
doubtedly intended to be fresh from the garden (or field).
Those modern cooks who must substitute dried herbs are

cautioned to use them sparingly. The general intention is, clearly, a green salad not very different from those we eat to-day, but with a rather larger component of the onion family than is usual in modern salads. It is advisable to be relatively sparing here, too: use only the smallest sort of leeks (if any are available) and onions. 'Garlic' may have meant the shoots or bulbs of wild garlic, which are much milder than the usual kind.

Green Salad

Salad greens: use an assortment of whatever greens are available, avoiding iceberg lettuce: in lieu of such rare greens as borage, you might try some spinach. Proportions of other ingredients below are predicated on a quantity of greens sufficient to fill one very large or two medium sized salad bowls.

1 tbsp each fresh (or 1 tsp dried) chopped parsley, sage, mint, and any other available, suitable herbs (eg, fennel, dill, savory)

1-2 bunches (depending on size and other ingredients) scallions, sliced

1-3 cloves garlic, minced

optional: 2-3 small leeks, well washed and finely sliced

optional: 2-3 tbsp chopped chives

1/2 cup salad oil (preferably olive oil)

3 tbsp vinegar

1 1/2 tsp salt

Wash and tear up greens. When well drained, put in bowl or bowls and add sliced scallions and leeks. Herbs, garlic, and oil may be added now, with the salt and vinegar reserved for the last minute, or, if you prefer, mix herbs, garlic, oil, vinegar, and salt as you normally would a salad dressing and add all at the same time just before serving: it comes to much the same thing. (It is the salt and vinegar which cause greens to wilt.) Mix and toss in the usual way.

45 Macrows

Take and make a thynne foyle of dowh, and kerve it on pieces, and cast hem on boilling water & seep it wele; take chese and grate it and butter cast bynethen and above as losyns, and serue forth. FC 92

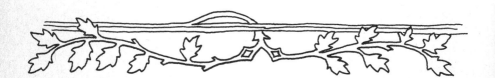

Noodles

1 lb broad noodles (homemade if you wish – see a standard cookbook)
1/4 cup (or more) grated cheese – cheddar, parmesan, or whatever you wish
2 tbsp butter (or more, to taste)

If your noodles are very long ones, break them into pieces a few inches in length. Boil in salted water until tender. In a serving dish or platter, put a layer of pieces of butter and half the cheese; put noodles on top of this; then add a second layer of butter and cheese, and serve hot.

VARIATION

Loseyns (lasagna) are made similarly, but presumably with larger noodles. FC 49 directs us to cook the Loseyns in broth (meat or chicken), then put them in a serving dish in several layers, with a layer of grated cheese and mild spices (eg, a mixture of cinnamon and mace – but be sparing with the spices) between layers. It is not clear whether any of the broth is poured over the completed arrangement, but it is probably not necessary and best omitted. If this does not seem much like a modern lasagna, remember that tomatoes were unknown in this period.

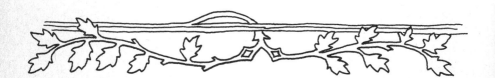

Fyssh

Some fish dishes have already been listed in the sections on soups and pottages and entremets; in this section we include primarily main-course dishes. The sauces given at the end may be used on almost any fish (steamed, fried, or broiled), as may those given with specific fishes in recipes; some of the sauces may also be used for meats and poultry.

46 ﬃyssh in Pottage

Take water and set it to boil with almonds in it; then peel and grind the almonds; moisten them with warm water; strain them and boil them with powdered ginger and saffron; and serve in bowls, and in each bowl put a slice of fried fish. MP

Most similar recipes call for broth or fish stock, which usually is laced with wine or vinegar. Such stock naturally gives the soup a lot more flavour.

Fish Soup

1 lb sliced fish (eg, cod or hake), plus some bones and
   trimming to make broth
4 cups water plus 1/4 cup vinegar, *or* 3 cups water plus
   1 cup white wine
1 tsp salt
1 oz ground almonds (or start with whole ones and blanch
   as directed in the recipe: it makes no difference)
1/4 tsp each ground ginger, saffron
2 tbsp olive oil

Cover the fish bones and trimmings with water, wine or vinegar, almonds, and seasonings, and simmer gently for about 20 minutes. Then fry the fish steaks in olive oil; they should be browned, but not overcooked to the point of becoming dry. Put a slice of fish in each serving bowl and strain the broth over it. Serve at once.

47 Ballok Brothe

'Pik and eles in ballok brothe/that muste our dame haue, or/els she will be wrothe.' To mak eles and pikes in ballok brothe take and splat a pik and shale hym and culpon eles smale and put them in a pot, do ther to grene onyons and qupbibes and mince them and sesson them up with a liore of bread and put to it clobes maces pouder of cannell and saffron and put ther to a quantity of stock fisches like unto the eles and let the pik boile esely and serue the hole pik for a lord and quarto of a pik for comons... N

All Ballok Broth recipes call for eels, in various proportions and combinations, but since not all cooks will be able to get eel easily today we assume you may use whatever fish you can get. One ingredient is omitted here which is usual in other versions: brewer's yeast, clearly included for the flavour.

Fish in Broth

1 lb fresh fish fillets or skinned slices, preferably including some eel, plus pike, pickerel, or cod
1/2 lb (ca) salt cod, soaked in cold water for at least 8 hours, with any skin and bone removed
1 cup (at least) chopped onions and/or green onions or scallions
1/4 cup chopped parsley
3-4 slices bread (white or whole wheat)
1 cup white wine
1/8 tsp each ground mace and cubebs or pepper
pinch each saffron, ground cloves
1 tsp vinegar
1 tbsp brewers' yeast

Cut fish (including soaked salt cod) into chunks. Put in a pot with onions, parsley, saffron, and four cups water; bring to a

boil and simmer gently for ten to fifteen minutes. Meanwhile, soak the bread (torn up or ground into crumbs) in wine. When it is well softened add all remaining seasonings and blend in a blender or mortar or press through a strainer. Stir this mixture into the soup with the yeast and cook, stirring, for about five more minutes.

48 Samon Roste in Sauce

Take a Salmond and cut him rounde, chyne and all, and roste the peces on a gredirne; And take wyne, and pouder of Canell, and drawe it þorgh a streynour; And take smale mynced oynons, and caste þere=to, and lete hem boyle; And þen take vynegre, or vergeous, and pouder ginger, and cast there=to; And þen ley þe samon in a dissh, and cast þe sirip þeron al hote, & serue it forth. HARL 4016

Grilled Salmon Steaks in Sauce

for 6 salmon steaks (around 3 lbs)
1 cup white wine
1/8 tsp (approximately) cinnamon
1 onion, or 3-4 green onions or scallions, finely minced
juice of 1/2 lemon or 1 tbsp vinegar
1/8 tsp (approximately) ginger
salt to taste

Broil the salmon steaks, after brushing them with some cooking oil or melted butter. Meanwhile, put onions or scallions in a saucepan with wine and cinnamon and bring to a boil; turn down heat and simmer gently. When salmon steaks are browned on both sides, add the lemon or vinegar and ginger to the sauce. Put salmon on a serving dish and pour the sauce over it.

49 Salmon Fressh Boiled

Take a fressh Salmon, and drawe him in þe bely; and
chyne him as a swyne, and leche him flatte with a knyfe; and
kutte the chyne in ii. or in iii. peces, and roste him on a faire
gredyrn; & make faire sauce of water, parcelly, and salt.
And whan hit begynneth to boyle, skem it clene, and cast þe
peces of salmon þere=to, and lete hem sethe; and þen take
hem vppe, and lete hem kele, and ley a pece or ii. in a dissh;
and wete faire foiles of parcely in binegre, and caste hem
vppon þe salmon in the dissh; And þen ye shall serue hit
forthe colde. HARL 4016

The principal difference here from modern practice is that
the salmon is grilled before it is poached: cooks must be careful to do both steps briefly, or it will be overcooked.

Cold Poached Salmon

1 salmon, head and tail off; cleaned and split, but not fileted
water, parsley, salt, and vinegar: in quantities appropriate to
  the size of the fish

Lay the salmon flat on a cutting board and cut it into two or
three pieces (depending on size) crosswise. Grill it in a broiler
or on a grill pan for about 5 minutes – just enough to make it
golden, not brown. Meanwhile, fill a shallow pan large enough
to hold the pieces of fish with water, salt, and a few sprigs of
parsley (ca 1 tsp salt to a quart of water); bring this to a boil,
and put in the salmon. Turn down the heat so that the water
barely simmers. Remove the fish in five minutes and let it
cool before arranging on a dish or platter for serving. Cover
and chill. When ready to serve the dish, take a good number
of small sprigs of parsley – enough to really make an impressive appearance – and dip each sprig in vinegar before arranging the parsley over the cold salmon.

50 Cawdel of Samon

Take the gutts of Samon and make hem clene; parboile hem a lytell; take hem up and dyce hem. Slyt the white of Lekes and kerue hem smale. Cole the broth and do the lekes þerinne with oile, and lat it boile togyder. Do the Samon icorne þerin; make a lyor of Almand mylke & of brede & cast þerto spices, safron, and salt; seeþ it wel, and loke þat it be not stondyng. FC 111

Salmon and Leeks in Almond Sauce

a chunk of salmon, ca 2 lbs (the tail-piece is usually most
   economical)
3-4 leeks
2 tbsp olive oil
2 oz (1/4 cup) ground, blanched almonds
ca 5 tbsp breadcrumbs
1/4 tsp ginger
1/8 tsp cinnamon
1/2 tsp salt
optional: pinch ground saffron

Poach the salmon in enough water to barely cover (ca 2 cups) for about 15 minutes; remove and allow to cool. Strain broth and measure 2 cups into a saucepan. Wash the leeks, and slice the white part finely into the broth in which the salmon was cooked; stir in oil, and bring to a simmer. When the leeks have been cooking about 15 minutes, add the salmon, skinned and cut into chunks about 1-2 inches square. Stir about 1/2 cup of the broth into the almonds and breadcrumbs, and beat until thoroughly dissolved; then mix back into the pot. If the mixture is not thick enough, add more breadcrumbs. Season, and allow to simmer over low heat for a few more minutes before serving. The dish should be on the runny side, like a creamed salmon.

51 Makerel in Mynt Sawse

Take Makerels and smyte hem on pecys; cast hem on water and berious; seep hem with myntes and wiþ ooþer erbes; color it grene or ȝelow, and messe it forth. FC 106

This recipe is especially recommended to those who think they do not care for mackerel: it has a subtly transforming effect on this inexpensive fish. While the recipe above calls for cutting the fish up, a later version leaves it whole, which may make a more attractive (if somewhat less convenient) dish.

Mackerel in Mint Sauce

2-3 mackerels, amounting to at least 2 lbs of fish
1 cup water, salted (use about 1/2 tsp salt)
1/4 cup vinegar (white vinegar has least discolouring effect)
4 large sprigs parsley and 3 or so of fresh mint
   (if you must use dried mint, ca 1 tbsp)
3-4 scallions or green onions

Mackerel should be cleaned and the head removed (though it may be left on if you wish to cook it whole). Leave whole or cut into pieces about two inches long. Put it in a cooking pot with the scallions, mint, and 3 of the parsley sprigs; pour salted water and vinegar over it and bring to a simmer. Cook gently for 15-20 minutes (depending on whether fish is whole or cut up). Remove fish to a serving dish. Sprinkle with remaining parsley, finely minced, and pour some of the cooking liquid, strained, over it. (Or use some sorrell, minced or ground with salt, in place of minced parsley for the sauce: this is specifically prescribed in the slightly later version.)

52 Roseye of Fysshe

Take Almaunde Mylke an flowre of Rys, & Sugre, an Safroun, an boyle hem y=fere; þan take Red Rosys, an grynd fayre in a morter with Almaunde mylke; þan take Loches, an toyle hem with Flowre, an frye hem, & ley hem in dysshys; þan take gode pouder, and do in þe Sewe, and cast þe Sewe a=boupn þe lochys, & serue forth. HARL 279.100

The roses used in this recipe can be ones that are just a bit too far gone to put (or keep) in a vase for decorative purposes; as long as they are not completely dried up, they will do.

Fish in Rose Sauce

2 lbs small fish or fish fillets
flour for dredging fish
oil for frying

SAUCE
2 tbsp plus 2 tsp ground almonds
4 tsp cornstarch, rice flour, or potato flour
2 tsp sugar
small pinch saffron
ca 1/2 cup red rose petals (1-2 roses)
1 cup water
1/2 tsp salt
1/8 tsp ginger

Flour and fry the fish, removing to a serving dish when done; keep warm. Make sauce at the last minute: it must not be overcooked or rewarmed after the roses are added. Dissolve starch in 2 tbsp cold water; add rest of water, sugar, 2 tbsp almonds, and saffron; boil and stir until thick; set aside. Grind rose petals with remaining almonds in morter (or use blender, or improvise), adding a bit of the cooked sauce.

When all is blended into a smooth paste, stir into the sauce base and reheat gently, just to the boiling point. Season with ginger and salt and strain over the fried fish.

53 Turbut Roste Ensauce

Take a Turbut, and kut of þe vynnes in maner of a haste=lette, and broche him on a rounde broche, and roast him; And whan hit is half y=rosted, cast thereon smale salt as he rosteth. And take also as he rosteth, vergeous, or vinegre, wyne, pouder of Gynger, and a litull canell, and cast thereon as he rosteth, And holde a dissh vnderneth, fore spilling of the licour; And whan hit is rosted ynowe, hete þe same sauce ouer the fire, And caste hit in a dissh to þe fissh all hote, And serue it forth. HARL 4016

Roast Turbot in Sauce

1 large turbot, skinned, or 2 fillets
1 tsp salt
1/4 tsp ginger
pinch cinnamon
2 tbsp lemon juice or vinegar

Grill the turbot in a broiler, with a pan underneath to catch the juices. When it is about half done (ca 10 minutes), mix together salt and spices and sprinkle this powder over the fish; sprinkle with lemon juice or vinegar and continue broiling. When fish is done, remove to a serving platter; rewarm the pan drippings if necessary (it probably will not be, in a modern broiler) and pour them over the fish.

54 Pike in Rosemarye

Put them to roast well on the griddle so that they are well cooked. For the sauce to put on them: red wine, verjuice, a very little vinegar, and some ginger and some rosemary, and cook them all to boil together in an earthenware pot; and when the pike are cooked, pour it over. MP, APP 5

Pike in Rosemary Sauce

1-2 whole pike (or pickerel), cleaned for roasting or split
  for broiling
1/2 cup red wine
2 tsp vinegar (wine or cider vinegar)
1/4 tsp each ginger, rosemary

Roast the pike by grilling in a broiler or over charcoal. While it cooks, mix the sauce ingredients and simmer over low heat for at least 10 minutes. (If too much of the wine evaporates, add a little water. But it should cook down a bit.) When the fish is done, salt it and pour the sauce over it on a serving platter.

55 Pike in Galentyne

Take browne brede, and stepe it in a quarte of vinegre, and a pynt of wyne for a pike, and quarteren of pouder canell, and drawe it thorgh a streynour skilfully thik, and cast it in a potte, and lete boyle; and cast there-to pouder peper, or ginger, or of clowes, and lete kele. And þen take a pike, and seth him in good sauce, and take him vp, and lete him kele a litul; and ley him in a boll for to cary him yn; and cast þe sauce vnder him and aboue him, that he be al y-hidde in þe sauce; and cary him wheþer euer þou wolt. HARL 4016

None of the English recipes for this dish is entirely satisfactory: thus the recipe below is largely based on a 14th century

Italian source, but we thought we would spare our readers the Latin. What does emerge from a comparison of the various recipes and sources of information is that this was usually a cold, jellied dish.

Galantine of Pike

1 whole (or large unskinned chunk of) fish, preferably pike or pickerel; 2-3 lbs
1 1/2 cups each white wine and water (use a little more water if necessary to cover fish)
1 onion, peeled and chopped
2 sprigs parsley
1/2 tsp salt
2 thin slices wholewheat bread, toasted
1 tbsp each wine vinegar, white wine
1/8 tsp each cinnamon, ginger, pepper, and (if you have any) galingale
pinch of ground clove

Cover the fish, onion, and parsley with wine and water; salt, and bring to a simmer. Cook gently 15-20 minutes, then remove fish and leave to cool. Boil down broth to about half its original quantity. Meanwhile, soak the bread and spices in wine and vinegar. Put the bread mixture in a blender, add some of the reduced broth, and blend. (If you have no blender, use a mortar, or whisk vigorously, then press through a strainer.) Add this paste to the rest of the broth and boil for a few minutes, or until thick, then set aside to cool. Remove skin from fish and put it in a dish: preferably one just large enough to hold it with sides two or three inches deep. Pour broth mixture over fish, turning the fish very gently to ensure complete coverage. Cool and chill. If the fish is not completely covered by sauce (and it will not be, unless you have a dish of exactly the right size and shape) you will need to ladle the sauce over the fish several times during the cooling period to make sure it is completely coated.

56 Stokfissh in Sauce

Take faire broth of elys, or pike, or elles of fressh samond, And streyn hit thorgh a streynour; and take faire parcelly, And hewe hem small, And putte the broth and þe parcelley into an erthen potte, And caste þerto pouder ginger, and a litul bergeous, And let hem boyle to-gidre; and þen take faire sodden stokfissh, and ley hit in hote water; and whan þou wilt serue it forth, take þe fissh fro þe water, and ley hit in a dissh, And caste the sauce al hote there=on, and serue it forth. HARL 4016

Salt Cod in Fish Stock

2 lbs dried salt cod (approximately)
bones and pieces of a white-fleshed fish or salmon to make
  fish stock (or use leftover stock from poaching salmon,
  pike, etc); about 1/4 lb, if you are buying pieces for the
  purpose, should be ample.
ca 1/4 cup finely minced parsley
1/4 tsp ground ginger
2 tbsp butter
2 tbsp lemon juice

Beat the dried cod by hitting against a table or counter top about a dozen times; this helps to soften the tissues of the fish when it is cooked. (Be thankful that you do not have to follow the Ménagier's directions to beat it with a wooden mallet for a full hour.) Soak the cod in water overnight – or at least 12 hours. Drain and add fresh, cold water; bring slowly to a boil and simmer gently for 5-10 minutes; then turn off heat and leave the fish in the water while you prepare sauce – or, remove from water, and recover with hot water for a few minutes to heat through just before serving.

If you have no leftover fish stock, make some by covering fish bones and pieces with water, boiling for about 20 minutes before straining. Measure one cup of this broth and put

it in a saucepan with the parsley, ginger, and butter. Bring to a boil, but cook for only a minute or two. Add lemon juice. Then drain the water from the cod, put it on a serving dish, and pour the sauce over it.

57 Cretone of Fyssh

Fish and Peas in Cream Sauce

Follow the recipe for Checones in Critone (88), but substitute ca 2 lbs fried fish (fillets of sole, cod, etc) for the chicken; ground almonds may be used in place of breadcrumbs (MP).

58 Blamanger of Fysshe

Take Rys, an sethe hem tylle they brekyn, & late hem kele; þan caste þer-to mylke of Almaundys; nym Perche or Lopstere & do þer-to, & melle it; þan nym sugre with pouder Gyngere, & caste þer-to, & make it chargeaunt, and þan serue it forth. HARL 279.98

Rice with Shellfish

4-6 lobster tails (depending on size)
1/2 lb raw medium shrimps
1 cup uncooked rice
4 oz (1/2 cup) ground blanched almonds
1/2 cup white wine
1 tsp sugar
1/2 tsp ginger
salt to taste

Cover the lobster tails and shrimps with salted, boiling water and parboil for 3-4 minutes. Pour the cooking water into another container and measure 1 cup of it; pour this cup of broth over the ground almonds and leave to steep 15-20 minutes.

Meanwhile, steam the rice in enough water to cover amply for 10-15 minutes; drain off any excess water. Shell the shrimps. Split the bottom of the lobster shells neatly in order to remove the meat but leave the shells in one piece. Cut the lobster meat and most of the shrimps into chunks, reserving a few of the shrimps and the lobster shells for later use. Stir the lobster and shrimp chunks into the rice with the seasonings and the almond milk and wine; add salt, if necessary. Stir this mixture over low heat for a few minutes. It should be thick and well-blended, but not dry. If it is on the dry side, add a little water. Pack into a ring-mold or casserole and cover with aluminum foil.

Just before serving, reheat in a moderate oven. Unmold onto a suitable tray or large plate, and decorate with the reserved lobster shells curling around the sides, or, if you have used a ring-mold, forming ribs from the middle to the outside; arrange the reserved shrimps between the lobster shells.

VARIATIONS
For an equally tasty, and far more economical, though obviously less spectacular, dish, use perch – or another kind of fish. One recipe suggests dried haddock, and, indeed, finnan haddie – or dried or smoked cod – will do very nicely. But when there are to be no lobster shells for decoration, there is little point in unmolding, and one might as well serve the dish from the casserole in which it is cooked.

59 Crustard of Eerbis

Take gode Eerbys and grynde hem smale with wallenots pycked clene, a grete portion; lye it up almost wiþ as myche berious as water; seeþ it wel with powdor and Safron withoute Salt; make a crust in a trap an do þe fyssh þerinne unstewed wiþ a litel oile & gode Powdors; whan it is half ybake do þe sewe þerto & bake it up. If þu wilt make it clere of Fyssh seeþ ayren harde take out þe ȝolks & grinde hem with gode powdors, and alye it up with gode stewes and serue it forth. FC 157

The recipe indicates that hardboiled egg yolks can be substituted for the fish, but should be mixed with the green sauce rather than put beneath it. This could be adapted in various ways: putting whole hardboiled eggs, or halves or quarters, under the sauce, for example. A sort of mixture seems, however, most appealing.

Quiche of Fish with Green Topping

about two handfuls (exact measurements are almost
   impossible for this small quantity of green stuff) of greens:
   a good combination is about 2/3 spinach, plus a few leafy
   tops of fennel (the bulb can be used separately – see, eg,
   Fenkel in Soppes (4), and the rest of the green part in
   salad), a few sprigs of parsley, and a green onion or scallion
   or two.
1/2 cup walnut meats
juice of 1 lemon
1 lb fish fillets (sole, flounder, perch, or what-have-you:
   the omission of salt in the 14th century directions indicates that stockfish (salt cod) was used, but for this recipe
   modern cooks will find fresh fish excellent.)
pastry to line a pie pan or baking dish
ca 1/8 tsp each ginger, cinnamon   *(more)*

1/2 tsp salt (or more, to taste)
1-2 tbsp olive oil or other cooking oil
2 yolks of hardboiled eggs

Line a suitable baking dish or piepan with pastry, fluting the top edge. Place the fish fillets in the bottom, and sprinkle oil and spices over them. Bake in a 350° oven for 10-15 minutes. Meanwhile, mince the greens and walnuts as finely as possible: it is best to put them through a meat grinder, or chop them in a blender with the lemon juice and an equal quantity of water. Put them in a saucepan with only this amount of liquid (that is, the juice of one lemon and an approximately equal quantity of water) and simmer for 4-5 minutes. Mash the egg yolks (or crush in a mortar); mix them into the cooked green sauce, and add salt to taste. Spread this mixture over the fish in the tart, and bake for another 10-15 minutes.

VARIATIONS
1 As suggested above, one could substitute hardboiled eggs for the fish for a dish with no fish or meat, with a larger proportion of greens.
2 Fish may be cooked this way in a shallow baking dish (oiled) without the crust.

60 **Tart of Fysshe**

Take Eelys and Samon and smyte hem on pecys; & stewe it in almand mylke and berious. Drawe up on almand mylk wiþ þe stewe. Pyke out þe bons clene of þe fyssh, and save þe myddell pece hoole of þe Eelys, & grynde þat ooþer fissh smale, and do þerto powdor, sugar, & salt and grated brede; & Fors þe Eelys þerwith þeras þe bonys were; medle þe ooþer dele of the fars & þe mylk togider, and color it with sanders: make a crust in a trap as before, and bake it þerin and serue it forth. FC 170

Since eel is not always available in fishmarkets, we offer here an alternative version (as well as directions for using eel).

Fish Tart

ca 1 lb eel, sliced, or fillets of sole (any sort of flounder, etc, will do)
ca 1 lb salmon (slices or chunk: whatever is the cheapest)
pastry to line a *large* pie plate or other shallow baking dish
1 tsp salt
4 oz (1/2 cup) ground almonds
juice of one lemon
one slice white bread (or ca 1/4 cup crumbs of same)
1/8 tsp each cinnamon, ginger; pinch of nutmeg
1/2 tsp sugar

Put lemon juice, salt, and 2 tbsp of the almonds in a cooking pot in which the fish will fit, and stir in a little water. Put the salmon and eel (if used: fillets should not be poached at this point) in the pot and add just enough more water to cover the fish. Bring to a simmer and cook gently for about ten minutes, then remove fish and allow to cool a few minutes. Strain broth and measure 1 1/2 cups (add water if necessary); stir the rest of the ground almonds into this broth and put it aside to steep while you line the baking dish with pastry and remove skin and bones from the poached fish. Put bread (torn, or in crumbs) in a blender container or bowl, and pour some of the almond milk over it (ca 1/2 cup); add the spices to this, along with the skinned, boned salmon, and blend, mash, or grind into a smooth thick paste.

If you are using fish fillets, cut them in half lengthwise to make strips about 1 1/2 to 2 inches wide. Roll these strips into round rings about 3 to 4 inches in diameter (with a hole about an inch in diameter in the middle), arranging these rings in the pastry crust. If using eel, it is easier to stuff the centres of the pieces of eel before putting them in the pie shell. In either case, then, stuff centres with salmon mixture. Then add the rest of the almond milk to the salmon that is left (which should be about half), and blend again. Pour this over the fish in the tart. Bake at about 325° for 40-50 minutes. Serve hot.

61 Verde Sawse

Take parsel, mynt, garlek, a litul serpell and sawge, a litul canel, gynger, piper, wyne, brede, vyneger & salt; grynde it smal with safron & messe it forth. FC 140

Green Sauce is the most common medieval (and later) accompaniment to fish: the recipes vary from very simple (parsley, ground with vinegar, bread, and salt) to infinite variations: besides the ingredients named in the 14th century recipe given here, recipes call for such other greens as sage, sorrel, ditteny, pellitory, and costmarye; spices may include cloves. The recipe suggested below can be varied infinitely, depending on what herbs you have on hand (and what spices you wish to try).

Green Sauce

2 tbsp fresh parsley, finely minced
2 tsp each fresh thyme, savory, and/or rosemary, finely
    minced (or, if need be, substitute rather less of dried herbs)
2 tbsp fine bread crumbs
1/2 tsp salt
1/8 tsp each ginger, pepper
1 tbsp lemon juice
1/4 cup white wine

Mix all ingredients together in a saucepan and stir over medium heat just long enough to thicken; do not overcook or sauce will loose its fresh, green quality. Or the sauce may be served without any cooking at all, if your crumbs are finely ground enough; since only a little sauce is needed, serving it cold will not cool the fish too much. Serve with poached, grilled, or sautéed fish.

62 Jance Sawce

*Grind ginger, garlic, almonds, and moisten with good ver-
juice, and then boil. And some put in a third part of wine.*

MP

The Ménagier recommends this sauce with cod and some
other fishes, as well as goose. Bread crumbs are an alternate
thickening; if you wish to omit them, increase the almonds.
Serve with steamed, fried, or broiled fish (cod, turbot, hali-
but, bluefish, etc).

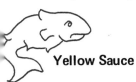

Yellow Sauce

2 tbsp ground almonds
3 cloves garlic, mashed
1/2 tsp each ginger, salt
juice of 1/2 lemon
1 cup white wine
2 tbsp bread crumbs

Mix all ingredients together in a saucepan; boil gently, stirring
or whisking well, until it thickens. Leave it on very low heat
to keep warm and mellow in flavour while you cook the fish;
or, set it aside for at least fifteen minutes, then reheat.

If your fish is to be cooked in wine and water, the stock
may be substituted for the white wine in the recipe; in this
case, the sauce may be made at the last minute and will not
need time to mellow.

63 Garlic Cameline

Grind ginger, garlic, and bits of white bread moistened with vinegar; and if you add liver to it it will be better. MP

The Ménagier recommends this sauce for fried ray or skate, but it can be used for other bland fried fish. It is quite possible that since this is called 'cameline,' cinnamon ought to be added: if you wish, add a pinch.

Garlic Cameline

1/2 tsp ground ginger
2 cloves garlic, mashed or put through a garlic press
1/4 cup bread crumbs (or 1 slice bread)
2 tbsp vinegar
1/4 tsp salt
optional: liver of the fish, chopped

Soak bread or bread crumbs with vinegar; put all ingredients in a small pan and cook, stirring, for a few minutes. If it seems too thick, add a little water or white wine. Serve hot with fried fish.

Rostes and
Bake Metes of Flessh

Since all cooks roast meat and poultry in standard ways, no directions will be given here for ordinary roasting procedures: medieval cookery books assume one knows that much. Follow your usual methods. The recipes included are for roasts with stuffings, sauces, etc; they include recipes for grilled meats, and meat pies, tarts, and 'crustards' – open tarts with a topping which crusts over in cooking.

64 Chik Y-rostyd with Sauce of Rose Water

In summer, the sauce for a roast chicken is half vinegar, half rosewater, and press ... orange juice is good added to this. MP

Oranges in the 14th century were bitter, not the sweet juice oranges familiar today. If you can get Seville oranges, they will be closest in flavour; otherwise, a combination of orange and lemon, or an adjustment in the amount of vinegar, is necessary. If you wish to make your own rosewater, the Ménagier directs us to dry the rose petals in the sun; afterwards, they are presumably boiled in distilled water. But, of course, you can buy rosewater in many shops.

Chicken with Rosewater Sauce

1 chicken, roasted
ca 1 tbsp each wine vinegar, rosewater, orange juice, and
 lemon juice (or whatever combination of the sweet and
 sharp you can muster)
salt to taste

Mix the sauce ingredients with juices from the roasting pan and pour over the chicken before serving.

65 Chike Endored

Take a chike, and drawe him, and roste him, and lete the fete be on, and take awey the hede; then make batur of yolkes of eyron and floure, and caste ther=to pouder of ginger, and peper, saffron, and salt, and pouder hit faire til hit be rosted ynogh. HARL 4016

The basic essential for gilding is yolk of egg, beaten. Any other ingredients are variable and optional; we find we prefer a plain egg-yolk gilding, as the taste of saffron, for example, can be a bit overwhelming.

Gilded Chicken

1 chicken, ca 3 lbs, dressed for roasting
2 egg yolks, beaten (do not substitute a whole egg here)
1/2 tsp salt
optional: small pinch of saffron

Roast the chicken, using a spit if you have one; baste with the pan drippings as the chicken roasts. About half an hour before the bird is done, brush it with beaten egg yolk seasoned with salt (plus the saffron, if desired); repeat the brushing once or twice, until chicken is done.

VARIATIONS

1 Chike Endored Y-farced: for a really impressive production – make a stuffing of a pound of ground veal or pork, or a mixture of the two, mixed with the minced (or ground) raw chicken liver from the chicken, plus a beaten egg, two tbsp grated cheese, and 1/8 tsp each pepper, ginger, and mace, plus 1/4 tsp salt. Put about half this mixture into the chicken and sew or skewer it closed. Form the rest into small meat balls, an inch or so in diameter. Poach the meatballs for about 10 minutes in a pot of simmering beef broth (or

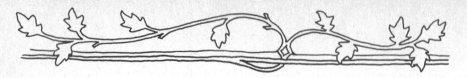

chicken, if you have no beef). Remove from the broth carefully, and thread on skewers. Put the skewered meat balls by the cooking chicken when it is time to gild the chicken, and gild the meat balls at the same time. To serve, arrange the meat balls as a decorative edging around the chicken on its platter. The French source of this recipe advises adding some parsley for a further decorative touch: the intention is minced parsley sprinkled on the balls, but a few sprigs tucked around them may be even more appealing to the eye.

2 Any number of other roasts – especially poultry – were gilded in the same way. Use the technique on anything that appeals to you. We assume, though, you will not get around to trying it on a peacock, that pièce de résistance for the ultimate in medieval feasts. One recipe reads: 'Take and flee off the skynne with the fedurs, tayle, and the nekke, and the hed thereon; then take the skyne with all the fedurs and lay hit on a table aborde; and strawe thereon groundyn comyn; then take the pecokke, and roste him, and endore hym with raw yolkes of egges; and when he is roasted take hym of, and let hym cool awhile, and take hym and sowe hym in his skyn, and gilde his combe, and so serve hym forthe with the last cours.' Needless to say, we have not kitchen-tested this technique.

Note: Sir Kenelm Digby (d 1665) reported, on the subject of roast chicken, 'The Queen useth to baste such meat with yolks of fresh Eggs beaten thin ...' but we rather doubt that 17th century gentry frequented the kitchen the way today's Jet Set is said to.

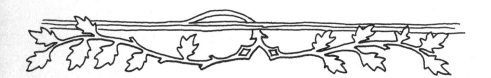

66 Capoun Ɏ-rostyde with Black Sauce

Take þe Lyuer of capouns, and roste hit wel; take anyse, and grynde parysgingere, and canel, and a litil cruste of brede, and grynde hit well all to-gedre; tempre hit up wiþ berious, and þe grece of the capon, þanne boile it and serue forþe. ASHMOLE 1439

This recipe is just as good for chicken as for capon, but, since a chicken is smaller, quantities should be halved.

Roast Capon or Chicken with Black Sauce

1 capon (ca 6 lbs)
1 capon liver
1/4 tsp each anise, ginger, cardamom, and cinnamon –
  all ground
ca 1/4 cup bread crumbs
1/2 tsp salt
2 tsp vinegar or lemon juice
ca 1 cup drippings from capon: if the quantity of drippings
  is insufficient, add some chicken (or capon) broth

Roast the capon in the usual way. Separately, roast the capon liver, or sauté it in a frying pan, until it is fairly well cooked, but not dried out. Crush or grind the liver (using a mortar or blender, if possible) with bread, vinegar, and other seasonings; put in a saucepan with the drippings and bring to a boil, stirring. Serve in a sauce dish or gravy boat along with the capon.

67 Gees with Sawse Madame

Take sawge, parsel, ysope, and sauary; quinces and peers,
garlek and Grapes, and fylle the gees þerwith; and sowe the
hole þat no grece come out. And roost hem wel, and kepe the
grece þat fallith þerof. Take galyntyne and grece and do in
a possynet, whan the gees buth rosted ynouh: take and
smyte hem on peeys, and þat tat is withinne and do in a
possynet and put þerinne wyne if it be to thyk. Do þerto
powdor of galyngale, powdor douce and salt; and boyle the
sawse, and dresse þe Gees in disshes, and lay þe sowe
onoward. FC 30

Goose with Sauce Madame

1 goose
1-2 tbsp each (less if dried) sage, parsley, hyssop (or mint),
 and savory
1 or 2 pears (hard; peeled, cored, and chopped)
1 or 2 quinces, if available (pared, cored, and chopped)
2-3 cloves garlic, mashed or finely minced
1 cup (approximately) seedless (or seeded) grapes
1/4 cup breadcrumbs
1/2 tsp cinnamon
1/4 tsp galingale or ginger
1/4 cup vinegar
1/4 cup red wine
1/2 tsp salt (or more, to taste)

Stuff the goose with a mixture of the fruits, herbs, and garlic;
sew or skewer closed, and roast on a rack in an open roasting
pan at 325° for 30 minutes per pound. Pour off the fat as it
accumulates, and set aside. When goose is about done, make a
sauce by blending together the breadcrumbs, vinegar, spices,
and wine, with a little of the accumulated fat (about 1/4 cup
is probably as much as most people would find palatable).

Pour the sauce over the goose, or serve separately.

VARIATIONS

1 Add chopped onions and the giblets of the goose to the stuffing. Omit quinces and garlic. When the goose is cooked, cut it up and arrange on a platter; put the stuffing in a pot with the other ingredients – using *white* wine and substituting, if you wish, several hardboiled yolks of eggs for the breadcrumbs; stir and simmer for a few minutes.

2 Omit quinces and pears. When goose is done, scoop out the stuffing and grind or mash it up with several yolks of hardboiled eggs and enough vinegar or lemon juice to make a thickish sauce. Omit spices.

3 The following variation is not really Sauce Madame, but it is a similar idea. Roast the goose unstuffed. When it is almost done, take 1/4 cup of the goose fat, 1 cup of red wine, 2 tbsp vinegar, 2 onions, minced, and/or 2 cloves of mashed garlic, and put in a pot with the goose giblets (parboiled and chopped), 1/2 cup currents, pepper, ginger, cinnamon, clove, and mace. Boil, stirring, and serve as a sauce for the goose.

68 Chawdon

Take þe lyuer and þe offall of the Swanns & do it to seeþ in gode broth; take it up, take out þe bonys; take & hewe the flessh smale; make a Lyor of crust of brede & of þe blode of þe Swan ysoden, & do þerto powdor of clows & of piper & of wyne & salt, & seeþ it & cast þe flessh þerto iþewed, and messe it forth with þe Swan. FC 143

Since swans rarely appear on the dining tables of England and North America, we have adapted the recipe by substituting duck. We also suspect most cooks will not have a sufficient supply of duck blood for the sauce, and thus suggest broth – with, if desired, a little gravy colouring.

Duck with Chawdon Sauce

1 duck, ready to roast, with neck and giblets
2 tbsp bread crumbs (whole wheat or other dark bread is best)
1/2 cup red wine
1/2 tsp salt
1 cup stock or broth (preferably brown chicken stock)
1/4 tsp pepper
1/8 tsp ground cloves
optional: a little gravy colouring

Put the heart, liver, gizzard, neck, and any residue of blood from the duck into a saucepan; cover with 1 cup stock or broth and bring to a boil. Turn down the heat, cover, and simmer. Remove liver and heart after 10 minutes; let the rest cook another 20 minutes, then remove with a slotted spoon and allow to cool. If the broth has not already boiled down to about 1/2 cup, boil it down to about that amount; strain and reserve.

Roast the duck as you usually roast duck. When it is almost done, proceed with the sauce. Discard any bones from the neck and grind all the meat (including liver, etc) cooked in the broth; if you use a blender, the sauce can be made in one step. To ground meat, add all other ingredients, including the reduced stock; when well blended, cook, stirring, for about five minutes, or until nicely thickened. Serve separately as a sauce for the duck.

69 Ffesaunte Rosteð

Lete a ffesaunte bloðe in þe mouthe as a crane, And lete him bleðe to dethe; pull him drp, kutte awep his heðe and the necke bp the boðp, and the legges bp the kne, and putte the kneps in at the bente, and roste him: his sauce is Sugur and mustarð. HARL 4016

Roast Pheasant

Sugar and mustard may sound a strange accompaniment to roast pheasant, and indeed some authorities of the period are firm that the pheasant should have no accompaniment but salt. However, the sugar and mustard combination may appeal to some tastes: if you wish to try it, mix powdered ground mustard with sugar and vinegar into a paste of fairly thin consistency. Or, substitute honey for sugar.

Pass separately with the roast pheasant: some diners are likely to prefer salt, alone, as advised by Wynken de Worde for roast fowl in general.

VARIATIONS
For game birds of all kinds, the *Modus Cenandi* recommends a cumin sauce. One given in the recipe for Checones in Critone (88 v1) would be suitable. Wynken de Worde suggests wine, ginger, and salt for partridge, and various combinations of wine or vinegar, ginger, pepper, mustard, and salt are specified elsewhere as sauces for game birds.

70 Rost Bef with Sauce Aliper

To mak sauce aliper for rostid bef take brown bred and stepe it in venygar and toiste it and strepne it and stampe garlic and put ther to pouder of pepper and salt and boile it a litill and serue it. N

This recipe has two defects: it reverses the order of toasting and steeping (it would be pretty hard to toast soaked bread) and it does not tell us to add any liquid except vinegar, although the sauce will have to be liquid enough to be boiled. But it has the great advantage of telling us what the sauce is to go with. The deficiencies are easily repaired by comparison with other recipes for the same sauce (which do not tell us what to serve it with), and other similar sauces.

Roast Beef with Garlic-Pepper Sauce

Roast beef (whatever cut you prefer and/or can afford,
   roasted as you like it)
2 slices wholewheat bread
2 tbsp wine vinegar
wine and/or stock, in quantities to produce desired
   consistency (see below)
2 cloves garlic, crushed
1/4 tsp each freshly ground black pepper, salt

When roast beef is almost ready to serve, toast the bread, then crumble it into a small bowl and pour the vinegar over it. Let this sit and soak for at least five minutes. Mash and put through a strainer, or blend in a blender. If you wish to make a boiled sauce (like a very thick gravy, with about 1 tbsp to be served with each slice of beef), add about 1 cup of beef stock and/or red wine; if, however, you wish to serve this as a very thick relish – rather like a modern horseradish sauce for beef – add only enough wine to make the paste of a soft consistency (up to 1/4 cup). Stir in garlic and seasonings,

tasting to see whether more salt seems called for. Serve as is if giving the thicker version, or, if making a thinner sauce, boil for a few minutes, and serve hot.

71 Venysoun Y-roste with Piper Sauce

𝔗ake brede, and frye it in grece, draw it up wiþ broþe and vinegre: caste þer-to poudre piper, and salt, sette on þe fire, boile it, and messe it forþ.   ASHMOLE 1439

This sauce is said to be a proper accompaniment to veal, goose, or venison – and some modern recipes for sauce for roast venison also make pepper a prominent spice. But John Russell advises salt and cinnamon with venison, and some of the modern recipes we have seen call for both pepper and cinnamon in a venison sauce. So we shall include both.

Roast Venison with Pepper Sauce

A roast of venison of ca 5 lbs (if unavailable, use veal)
3 slices white bread (crusts removed)
1 tbsp butter, lard, or beef fat
2 cups beef broth
1 tbsp wine vinegar
1 tsp salt
1/2 tsp each pepper, cinnamon

Roast the venison as you would beef, to the medium-well-done stage. (If the venison is old and tough, it should be marinated for several days beforehand, but young venison needs no marinade.) When it is about ready to serve, heat the butter (or other fat) in a frying pan and lightly fry the slices of bread. Pour over the bread a little of the broth (hot) and allow to soak for a few minutes. Then blend in remaining broth and all other ingredients – preferably in a blender. Boil the sauce, stirring, until thickened; serve separately.

72 Stepkys of Venson or Bef

Take Venyson or Bef, & leche & gredyl it vp broun; þen take Vynegre & a litel verious, & a lytil Wyne, & putte pouder perpir þer=on y=now, and pouder Gyngere; & atte þe dressoure straw on pouder Canelle y=nowe, þat þe stekys be al y=helid þer=wyth, & but a litel Sawce; & þan serue it forth. HARL 279.II.31

Venison was obviously the preferable, aristocratic, meat: beef, a poor substitute. Most of us will have to make do with beef these days. It is probable, however, that this recipe does more for venison than it does for good beef; many modern recipes for venison still specify sweet, spicy seasonings not so far from this model. It is still a good recipe for beef steaks, however, if one is reasonably restrained in the matter of cinnamon: few 20th century diners would fancy their beefsteaks completely covered with cinnamon powder.

Venison or Beef Steaks

2 lbs beef (or venison) steaks; a thick piece of flank steak (London Broil) which can be sliced on the bias before saucing is ideal
1 tbsp vinegar
2 tbsp red wine
1/2 tsp salt
1/4 tsp pepper
1/8 tsp each ginger and cinnamon (use more cinnamon if you are using venison rather than beef – or if you yearn for more authenticity)

Grill the steak either in a grill pan (one with ridges) or a slightly greased frying pan or under a broiler. Grill as long as

necessary, according to size and thickness, and remove from the heat onto a serving platter as soon as brown. Then mix together the vinegar, wine, and seasonings, and spoon over the steaks. Serve at once.

This is obviously not a dish to do ahead of time and then heat up: it is better saved for one's smaller feast occasions. Those who choose to try a larger proportion of cinnamon may leave it out of the sauce mixture and, instead, sprinkle it directly on the meat before pouring on the sauce. If these are done in a grill pan, or under a broiler, the juices from cooking may be saved and used for final seasoning of a vegetable: Gourdes (15), for example.

VARIATION
Use a tougher cut of meat, such as a chuck steak; brown quickly in a frying pan with a little butter or other fat, then add seasonings, turn the heat down to barely warm, cover, and leave to finish cooking for about half an hour. This variety may be easier to reheat, if that is a consideration.

73 Alows de Beef

Take fayre Bef of þe quyschons, & motoun of þe bottes, & kytte in þe maner of Stekys; þan take raw Percely, & Oynonys smal y-schredde, & 3olkys of Eyroun soþe hard, & Marow or swette, & hew alle þes to-geder smal; þan caste þer-on poudere of Gyngere & Saffroun, & tolle hem to-gederys with þin hond, & lay hem on þe Stekys al a-brode, & caste Salt þer-to; þen rolle to-gederys, & putte hem on a round spete, & roste hem til þey ben y-now. Þan lay hem in a dysshe and pore þer-on Vynegre & a lityl verious, & pouder Pepir þer-on y-now, & Gyngere, and Canelle, & a

fewe зolkуs of harд Eproun у=krempд þer=on; & serue forth.

Stuffed Beef Rolls

for 4 thin slices of steak (3/4 lb to 1 lb)
1 tbsp finely minced parsley
1 onion, minced
1 or 2 boiled eggs (or yolks only)
1 tbsp bone marrow, butter, or other cooking fat
1/4 tsp each ginger, salt
optional: small pinch ground saffron
juice of 1/2 lemon or 1 tbsp vinegar
sprinkling (scant) of pepper, ginger, cinnamon

Mix together parsley, onion, one egg yolk (mashed) or one whole boiled egg (chopped small) with marrow or fat, ginger, salt, and, if you wish, saffron. Spread this mixture on the steaks; then roll them up, securing with toothpicks and/or string (a combination is the best expedient). Put on skewers, for easy turning, and broil for about 10-15 minutes, turning to brown all sides of the rolls. When they are nicely browned, put them on a serving dish and sprinkle over them the lemon juice or vinegar, a dusting of pepper, ginger, and cinnamon, and crumbled yolk of hardboiled egg.

VARIATION

As the recipe suggests, lamb steaks may also be prepared in this fashion. Unless your butcher can provide you with bone-less, thin lamb steaks, try using slices from a leg, removing the bone with a sharp knife. If slices of lamb leg are too thick to be rolled, they should be sliced into thinner slices: this is not difficult to do if the meat is partially frozen.

74 Bourbelier de Sanglier

First put the loin in boiling water, then take it out and stick it all over with cloves. Set it to roast, basting it with a sauce made from spices: that is, ginger, cinnamon, clove, grains, long pepper, and nutmeg, moistened with verjuice, wine, and vinegar; and baste with this without first boiling it. And when the roast is done, boil together. MP

This recipe apparently calls for a loin of wild boar; but, since wild boars will not be found in the average North American market, we have substituted pork. Those who want something which more closely approximates the flavour of wild boar can try marinating the pork for a few days in a marinade of wine, vinegar, oil, and herbs: which procedure is supposed to render the flavour more like that of wild boar. However, the roast is a very tasty one without such preliminaries.

Loin of Pork in Boar's Tail Sauce

4-6 lb loin roast of pork
cloves (enough to stud the roast at 1 or 2 inch intervals)
1/2 tsp each ground ginger, cardamom, pepper, salt
1/4 tsp each cinnamon, ground cloves, nutmeg
1/4 cup wine (preferably red)
1 cup vinegar

Stick whole cloves into the loin of pork; mix together all other ingredients and pour over the pork. Roast in the usual way, basting from time to time. When the roast is done, pour off pan juices and boil together to make the sauce.

Some recipes call for a thickening of breadcrumbs; if such a thickening is desired, use about 2 tbsp crumbs, stirred in as the sauce is boiling.

75 Cormarye

Take Colyandre, Caraway smalle gronden, Powdor of Peper and garlec ygronde in red wyne; medle alle þise togyder and salt it; take loyn of Pork rawe and fle of þe skyn, and pryk it wel with a knyf, and lay it in þe sawse; roost þerof what þu wilt, & kepe þat fallith þerfro in þe rosting and seeþ it in a possynet with faire broth, & serue it forth with þe roost anoon. FC 53

This recipe consists of a savory sauce, with which a loin of pork is to be basted, the dripping to be used as a sauce for the pork.

Roast Pork with Caraway Sauce

5-7 lb pork loin roast
2-3 cloves garlic, crushed
1/2 to 1 tsp each coriander and caraway seed
1 cup red wine (or 1/2 cup, if using a clay baker)
1/2 tsp salt
1/4 tsp pepper

Ideally, use a coffee grinder for grinding seeds. If you have none, use a mortar, a blender (not all blenders will do this well), or a rolling-pin, with the seeds between two sheets of waxed paper. When they are crushed, mix with all other sauce ingredients, preferably in a blender. The more finely the spices and garlic can be ground, the more effective the sauce will be.

Prick the loin of pork all over and place in a rack over a roasting pan. Pour the sauce over it and roast in the usual way, basting with the juices in the pan from time to time plus, if it seems desirable, wine. (You may, of course, adapt this to clay-baking procedures, if you have a clay baker.) When roast is done, pour off the drippings into a saucepan and add a small amount of broth or stock (chicken stock,

preferably – or broth made from pork bones). Stir and bring to a boil; thicken if you wish. Serve as a sauce for the pork.

76 Mouton Y-rosted with Sawse Camelyne

Take Raysons of Corance, & kyrnels of notys, & crusts of brede & powdor of gynger, clowes, flour of canel; bray it wel togyder and do it þerto. Salt it, temper it up with vynegar, and serue it forth. FC 144

Cameline Sauce, like many other well-known dishes, varies from one recipe to another, though all contain cinnamon; this one is especially good, resembling a sort of chutney, which goes well with roast meat. The Ménagier suggests Cameline sauce with roast veal and rabbit, as well as with lamb, and tells us that both rabbit and veal should be parboiled and larded before roasting. It would be well to follow this advice if you wish to substitute one of them for the lamb.

Roast Lamb with Cameline Sauce

leg of lamb, roasted in the usual way
1/4 cup each currants and chopped nuts
   (walnuts are excellent)
2 tbsp breadcrumbs
1/2 tsp each ginger and cinnamon
1/4 tsp ground cloves
1/2 tsp salt (or more, to taste)
1/3 cup vinegar, preferably wine vinegar

If you have a blender, put all sauce ingredients in at once and blend until nuts and currants are finely chopped. Otherwise, a mortar may be used, or the currants and nuts chopped finely by hand and then mixed with other ingredients. Serve cold, in a separate dish. (*more*)

Some medieval directions call for sprinkling the roasting lamb with sage or thyme; others recommend dusting it with parsley as a finishing touch.

If a more liquid cameline is desired, add more vinegar. Or, for a simpler version, omit currants and nuts; wine may then be substituted for the vinegar, in which case the sauce should be boiled.

77 Longe de Buf

Nym the tonge of the rether and schalde and schawe yt wel and rizt clene, and seth yt, and sethe nym a broche and larde yt wyth lardons and wyth clowys and gelofer, and do it rostyng, and drop yt wel yt rostyd wyth zolkes of eyrin and dresse it forth. AC 43

While the larding technique is probably a very good idea, it is one many modern cooks do not normally bother with, so our recipe is somewhat adapted here. Adepts with the larding needle are, however, urged to lard properly.

Roast Tongue

1 tongue, fresh or canned
ca 6 strips fresh fat pork; or, bacon, parboiled and drained
cloves (whole)
2 egg yolks (raw) – one will be enough for a small canned
    tongue

Parboil the tongue in water for about 2 hours, if fresh. Peel, stud with cloves, and wrap in the pork strips (or parboiled bacon). Roast in a 350° oven for about an hour. After 45 minutes, remove the pork and brush with beaten egg yolk.

(The tongue may be roasted on a spit instead, of course; in this case, the pork larding will have to be skewered on firmly, or tied with string.)

VARIATIONS
The French recipe is identical, but omits the gilding. It also recommends a cameline sauce as an accompaniment to tongue; the sort of sauce probably intended is made of ginger, cinnamon, nutmeg, and breadcrumbs, moistened with cold water and wine or vinegar, but the cameline recipe given here as an accompaniment to lamb would be very good with tongue, too. (See Mouton Y-rosted with Sawse Camelyne (76).) The Ménagier also notes that salted tongues may be simply boiled in wine and water and eaten with mustard.

78 Chicken Pasties Lombard

Chicken may be set in a pasty on their backs with the breast upward and large slices of bacon on the breast, and then covered. Item: in the Lombard manner, when the chickens are plucked and prepared, take beaten eggs, both the yolks and the whites, with verjuice and spice powder, and dip your chickens in this; and set them in the pasty with strips of bacon, as above. MP

As a whole chicken in pastry is a problem in carving – unless the chicken is boned, a chore few cooks are prepared to execute – we have limited ourselves to breasts of chicken for this dish. The pasties are much neater if the breasts are boned, but that is not particularly difficult. (Save the bones as an ingredient for broth or stock.) If it seems desirable to serve these as appetizers, simply cut the breasts in two or more portions.

Chicken Pasties Lombard

4 boned chicken breasts (for four main course portions)
1 egg, beaten
1 tbsp lemon juice
1/2 tsp ginger
pinch each cinnamon, cloves, cardamom
2-4 slices bacon
pastry, plain or puff: full recipe

If regular breakfast bacon is to be used, cook it partially first to take out some of the fat; or use back bacon (Canadian bacon), which has little fat. Roll out pastry and divide into 4 equal parts before it is completely rolled out; then try to make each portion as round as possible as you finish rolling it out piece by piece.

Mix beaten egg, lemon juice, and spices, and dip the pieces of chicken in this mixture. Lay each piece on one side of a round of pastry with a slice of bacon on top; bring other half of pastry round over to cover, and pinch edges together. For a neatly finished effect, press a fork around the edges to flute. Bake in a 350° oven for 30-40 minutes, depending on size; if using puff pastry, the oven should be hotter and the time not so long.

VARIATION

For a larger and much more spectacular dish, substitute a whole frozen boned turkey roll (thawed) for the chicken breasts; use puff pastry and glaze with beaten egg (or egg white). Do not cook the bacon very much beforehand, as the turkey needs the extra fat. Purists may object on the grounds that there were no turkeys in medieval Europe (the first ones arrived in the 16th century), but then perhaps purists will be prepared to bone their own chickens.

79 Pies of Parys

Take and smyte faire buttes of porke and buttes of vele togidre, and put hit in a faire potte, And putte thereto faire broth, And a quantite of Wyne, And lete all boile togedidre til hit be ynogh; And þen take hit fro the fire, and lete kele a litel, and cast ther=to raw yolkes of eyren, and pouudre of gyngeuere, sugre and salt, and mynced dates, resepns of corence; make then coffyns of feyre past, and do it ther=ynne, and keuere it & lete bake y=nogh. HARL 4016

Other similar recipes suggest that the meats were variable, so we suspect a standard 'meat-loaf' mix, if your market carries one, will be fine. If you wish to serve as small hors d'œuvres, rather than as a main course, the same filling may be put into small tart shells, and, preferably, baked with a covering of aluminum foil, to be removed at the last moment, instead of a top crust: such small tarts will, of course, take less time to cook. In any case, however, it is advisable to do the parboiling of the meats well in advance of the rest of the cooking: modern tastes will prefer a de-fatted version, and it is a lot easier to remove the fat from the cooking juices if they are cooled for a time (even in a freezer, if you're in a real hurry).

Paris Pies

Pastry for a 9-inch pie pan (top and bottom) or
  ca 24 tart shells
1 1/2 lbs mixed ground meat, including at least two of
  pork, veal, beef
1 cup each meat stock or broth, red wine
3 egg yolks or 1 whole egg plus one yolk
1/2 tsp each ginger, sugar & salt
1/4 cup each minced dates, currants
optional: pinch of ground pepper or cubebs, and/or
  mace, ground clove

Put the ground raw meat in a saucepan and cover with the wine and water; bring to a boil and simmer for 10 minutes. Then drain all the cooking juices into a heatproof container, setting aside the meat. Let the cooking liquid cool (preferably in the refrigerator or freezer) until you can remove all the fat from the top.

When you are ready to assemble the pie, line a pie dish with pastry. Then bring the de-fatted juices to a boil; beat the egg yolks (or egg and yolk) in a bowl, and beat in a little of the hot (but not quite boiling) stock. Beat in the rest, still off the heat; then mix together meat, dried fruits, spices, and sauce, and stir over low heat for a few minutes to thicken slightly. Put in the prepared pie shell and cover with a top crust (unless you are making individual tarts). Bake in a pre-heated 350° oven for about one hour (less for individual tarts). As the mixture may tend to be pretty sloppy at first, be sure to slit the top crust to allow steam to escape; and it may also be wise to put a cookie sheet or piece of foil under the pie pan.

80 Mylates of Pork

Hewe Pork al to pecys and medle it with apren & chese igrated. Do þerto powdor fort, safron, & pyneres with salt; make a crust in a trap, bake it wel þerinne, and serue it forth. FC 155

Pork Tart

1/2 lb minced or ground pork
4 eggs, beaten
1/4 cup grated cheese (parmesan is fine)
pinch each nutmeg, ginger, cardamom, pepper
scant pinch saffron
1/2 tsp salt
pastry tart shell (uncooked)

Mix together meat, cheese, eggs, and seasonings, and put in tart shell. Bake at 375° for 45 minutes. The tart may be served cold, but it is better hot.

81 Grete Pyes

Take faire yonge beef, And suet of a fatte beste, or of Motton, and hak all this on a borde small; And caste thereto pouder of peper and salt; And whan it is small hewen, put hit in a bolle, And medle hem well; then make a faire large Cofyn, and couche som of this stuffur in. Then take Capons, Hennes, Mallardes, Connynges, and parboile hem clene; take wodekokkes, teles, grete briddes, and plom hem in a boiling potte; And then couche al þis fowle in þe Coffyn, And put in euerych of hem a quantite of pouder of peper and salt. Then take mary, harde yolkes of egges, Dates cut in ii. peces, reisons of coraunce, prunes, hole clowes, hole maces, Canell, and saffron. But first, when thou hast cowched all thi foule, ley the remenaunt of thyne other stuffer of beef abought hem, as þou thenkest goode; and then strawe on hem this: dates, mary, and reysons, etc., And then close thi Coffyn with a lydde of the same, And putte hit in þe oven, And lete hit bake ynogh; but be ware, or thou close hit, that there come no saffron nygh the brinkes there=of, for then hit wol neuer close. HARL 4016

While few modern cooks will want to do anything on such a grand scale as this recipe suggests, even for feeding a mob, a scaled-down version is quite legitimate: Mrs Napier's recipe, for example, calls for capon or pheasant, not a whole lot of different fowls, whole or in pieces. The recipe below is for a fairly large pie (baked in a 9 to 10 inch dish), with ingredients selected from several recipes; those who wish to do something grander can add more poultry and, if they have a suitable dish, make a really 'great' pie.

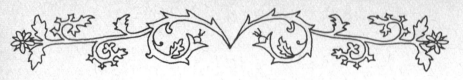

Great Pies

Pastry to make two crusts for large pie pan
1 lb ground beef
1/3 cup red wine
2 Cornish game hens *or* one frying chicken, cut up; *or*
  2 chicken breasts (large), split
1/4 cup each chopped dates, currants, prunes
1/2 tsp salt
1/4 tsp each mace, cinnamon
1/8 tsp each ground cloves, cubebs or pepper
optional: pinch of saffron (or turmeric); marrow, egg yolks

Parboil the poultry for five minutes in salted, boiling water; allow to cool and remove skin. If using breasts of chicken, pull out as many bones as possible while leaving the pieces reasonably whole. Line pie pan with pastry. In a large mixing bowl, mix all remaining ingredients; if it seems too dry and crumbly, add a bit more wine; spread a layer of half this mixture on the bottom of the pie shell, then arrange the poultry on top; spread the rest of the meat mixture over the poultry, cover with a crust, and slit to let steam escape. Bake in a 325° oven for about 1 hour and 10 minutes, or until nicely browned. Glazing the top by brushing it with beaten egg white before baking produces a nice effect: and those who have been using recipes calling for egg yolks may find plenty of extra egg white for this purpose.

Stewes

Under this section are collected hearty, stewed, braised, and boiled dishes, all of which would have come under the vague heading of 'pottages' for our ancestors. At medieval feasts dishes of this kind were served along with roasts or in following courses, depending on the elaborateness of the menu. Fish stews can be found in the section on fish.

82 Lorengue de Pouchins

Take the oranges and slice them in white verjuice and white wine, and put them to boil, and put in ginger; and put your poultry to cook in this. MP, APP 5

Oranges were not much used in England at this period, but were apparently known there; since the oranges were bitter – of the Seville type – the normal oranges available in North America will need some extra tartness for this dish. The recipe does not tell us exactly how to cook the chicken (one doubts that the cooking is intended to be entirely accomplished in the sauce), so we shall take it as a way to finish partly roasted chicken.

Chicken in Orange Sauce

1 chicken, roasted (but not quite done)
2 oranges, sliced but not peeled
1 cup white wine
juice of 1/2 lemon (omit if you are using bitter oranges)
1/4 tsp ginger
1/2 tsp salt (or to taste)

When chicken is almost done, put sauce ingredients in a pan and cook together about 15 minutes. Cut up the chicken into serving pieces and arrange it in a heat-proof serving dish; pour the sauce over it, cover with aluminum foil (if your dish has no cover) and simmer for another 15 minutes before serving.

The recipe states that this is also a sauce for partridge or pigeons.

If you prefer, the chicken or other poultry may be broiled or sautéed instead of roasted.

83 Schyconys with þe Bruesse

Take half a dosyn Chykonys, & putte hem in=to a potte; þen putte þer=to a gode gobet of fressh Beef, & lat hem boyle wel; putte þer=to Percely, Sawge leuys, Sauerey, noȝt to smal hakkyd; putte þer=to Safroun y=now; þen kytte þin Brewes & skalde hem with þe same broþe; Salt it wyl.

HARL 279.144

Comparison of this recipe with the Ménagier's Trumel de Beuf au Jaunet makes it evident that the beef to be used is the leg, and that this is, thus, chicken cooked with marrow-bones – the dish for which Chaucer's Cook was known. (The French recipe emphasizes the beef, but is otherwise the same.) Neither recipe calls for 'galengale' or 'pouder marchant,' but it would hardly be surprising if various spices were added by cooks. One almost indentical 16th century recipe calls for mace and ginger, among other things. In lieu of those mentioned in Chaucer's General Prologue, we feel a little experimentation with ginger and pepper is appropriate here. *Brewis* means toast used as a sop. Slices of toasted French bread are delicious with this dish – especially if it is really good French bread. The result is clearly the ancestor of a modern Pot au feu, or potée Normande.

Chickens with Brewis

1 roasting chicken, tied to keep its shape
ca 2 lbs beef shin (cracked, ie, sliced by the butcher)

water to cover meats (but use a pot as small as possible)
1 onion, peeled
2-3 sprigs parsley
ca 2 sprigs each sage, savory (1/4-1/2 tsp dried)
pinch saffron (not too small; the saffron is really needed here)
1 tsp salt (or more, to taste); pepper, ginger, as desired
small loaf French bread, sliced and lightly toasted

Put chicken, beef, and all seasonings in a pot; cover with water and simmer for about two hours. To serve, put slices of toast on serving platter and chicken in the middle, with beef around the chicken. Strain broth over the whole platter, being sure to soak the brewis well.

84 Gelyne in Dubbatte

Take an Henne, and rost hure almoste y=now, an choppe hyre in fayre pecys, and caste her on a potte; and caste þer=to Freysshe broþe, & half Wyne; Clowes, Maces, Pepir, Canelle; an stepe it with þe Same broþe fayre brede & Vynegre: and whan it is y=now, serue it forth. HARL 279.41

Perhaps the title of this dish is equivalent to the modern term 'en daube.' Note that a hen is called for: if you wish to use an older, tougher chicken, simply double the cooking time suggested, and increase (slightly) amounts of other ingredients, since the chicken will be larger.

Chicken in White Wine Sauce

1 chicken
1 1/2 cups each chicken broth, white wine
1/4 tsp each mace, cinnamon
1/8 tsp (or less) each ground cloves, pepper

1/2 tsp salt, or to taste
1/4 cup bread crumbs
2 tsp vinegar

Roast the chicken in a hot oven (ca 450°) for half an hour,
then cut it into serving pieces; or, cut it up first, and brown
in a little fat in a frying pan. Then put the chicken pieces in
a cooking pot or casserole, and add wine, broth, and spices.
Simmer for half an hour; then take a little of the cooking
broth, plus the vinegar, and mix the breadcrumbs into a
smooth paste. Add this to the pot, and stir over medium heat
to thicken.

85 Mawmenny

Take þe chese and of Flessh of capons or of henns, &
bakke smal and grynde hem smale in a morter. Take mylke
of Almands with þe broth of freissh Beef, oþer freissh
flessh, & put the flessh in þe mylke oþer in the broth and
set hem to þe fyre, & alye hem up with flour of Ryse or
gaftbon or ampdon as chargeant as þe blanke desire, &
with ȝolks of ayren and safron for to make it ȝelow. And
when it is dressit in disshes with blank desires styk aboue
clows de gilofre & strewe Powdor of galyngale aboue, and
serue it forth. FC 194

This recipe is presented in more than one source as to be
accompanied by what is here called 'blank desire' – variously
spelled elsewhere, but we shall call it Blandissorye: a sauce of
almonds mixed with broth, basically, though many other ingredients occur. But since the Mawmenny itself is made with
a similar sauce, most modern cooks will probably think the
extra sauce unnecessary. Those who wish to serve it in the
way here specified, however, should see the recipe for Blandissorye (5). They are advised to make the Mawmenny somewhat thicker than is specified here, so that it can be accompanied logically by the extra sauce.

Minced Chicken in Cheese and Almond Sauce

2-3 cups cold cooked chicken or capon, minced
1/2-2/3 cup minced or grated cheese (a mixture of
   Gruyere and Romano or Parmesan is pleasant)
2 tbsp ground almonds
2 cups chicken broth
2 tbsp rice flour or cornstarch
2 tbsp white wine
2 tbsp water
2 egg yolks (or one whole egg)
1/2 tsp salt
pinch of saffron
ca 1/4 tsp ground galengale or ginger

Steep the almonds in the broth for about 20 minutes. Dissolve rice flour or cornstarch in wine and water. Beat egg yolks (or egg). Heat the minced chicken and cheese in the almond milk; stir in rice flour mixture, with ground saffron, and stir until whole mixture is thick enough. Remove from heat and stir a little of the sauce into the beaten egg; then add this to the pot and stir, off the heat or over very low heat, for a few minutes. (Do not allow it to boil after adding the egg.)

   Pour into a suitable serving dish and sprinkle with galingale or ginger, and, if you wish, ground cloves.

VARIATION
Omit cheese; this ingredient appears only in one early recipe. One cheese-less recipe also omits eggs, and adds further seasonings: sugar, cinnamon, mace, cubebs, and anise.

86 Chykens in Hocchee

Take parsel and sawge withoute eny oþer erbes; take garlec
and grapes and stoppe þe Chikens ful, and seeþ hem in
gode broth, so þat þey may esely be boyled þerinne. Messe
hem and cast þerto powdor dowce. FC 34

Stuffed Boiled or Braised Chickens

1 roasting chicken
ca 1 cup (more-or-less: depending on the size of the chicken)
  seedless or seeded white grapes
ca 2 cloves garlic, mashed
ca 2 tbsp each parsley, sage (less sage if dried), finely minced
1-4 cups chicken broth (see below)
pinch each cinnamon, ginger, sugar, mixed with 1/2 tsp salt

The chicken may be boiled without any pre-browning, in
which case you will need enough broth to cover it (up to 4
cups), but we advise browning it in a little oil or fat in a frying pan first, in lieu of the usual medieval practice of roasting
the meat just long enough to brown it: or, even better, use an
unglazed clay pot, which will boil and brown at the same
time. In the latter case, use no more than 1 cup of broth.

In any case, mix together the grapes, garlic, parsley, and
sage, and stuff the chicken with this mixture. Skewer or tie
the chicken so that it is tightly closed and will hold its shape.
Put it in a cooking pot in which it will barely fit – or a clay
baker or a casserole – and pour the boiling broth over it. Simmer or bake (ca 350° oven, but you may adapt to your usual
practice with a clay baker, if you are using one) for about an
hour, or until done.

To serve, remove chicken from broth, and cut away string
or remove skewers. If it has not been browned, remove skin.
Sprinkle the spice powder over it and pour on a little of the
broth as a sauce. A spoonful of stuffing should, of course, be
served with every helping of meat.

87 Rosee of Hennys

𝔗ak the flowris of Rosys and wasch hem wel in water and after bray hem wel in a morter and than tak Almondys and temper hem and seth hem and after tak flesch of capons or of hennys and hac yt smale and than bray hem wel in a morter, and than do yt in the Rose so that the flesch accorde wyth the mylk and so that the mete be charchaunt, and after do yt to the fyre to boyle and do thereto sugur and safron that yt be wel ycolowrd and rosy of lebys and of the forseyde flowrys and serbe yt forth. AC 41

Exotic as this dish may sound, it is quite simple and pleasant, and to be recommended when you have some roses beginning to fade or wilt in the garden (or in a vase). We think it unwise to include saffron: the flavour can overwhelm the more delicate taste of the roses, and the colour added is more on the orange side than properly 'rosy.' If you want a more pronounced rose colour, add a drop or two of red food colouring.

Minced Chicken in Almond and Rosepetal Sauce

ca 3 cups diced cooked chicken
1 1/2 cups chicken broth
1 1/2 cups rose petals, red or pink (rinsed in cold water, dried gently, and with the white bases cut off; this amount means three or four roses of medium size)
2 oz (1/4 cup) chopped, slivered, or ground blanched almonds
1 tsp salt
optional: 1/2 tsp sugar, pinch of saffron

Put the rose petals in a mortar or coffee grinder with almonds – they are very difficult to grind by themselves. Since the average coffee grinder or small mortar will not hold this much, it will probably have to be done in 3 or more batches

of almonds and petals. Mix the resulting powder with the chicken broth (hot) and allow to steep for about ten minutes, or put in a saucepan and bring to a boil for a minute or two. Mince or grind the chicken as finely as possible and stir it into the sauce, or (preferably) blend it all together in a blender. Season and heat, stirring, for no more than five minutes. Do not overcook, or both flavour and colour will deteriorate.

To serve, mound on a serving dish or platter. It is good served with rice cooked in chicken broth with saffron, which can form a border on the serving dish. For an authentic decorative touch, garnish with a few more rose petals. (They taste like a really superior lettuce.)

This dish is also excellent cold, and may be served as a sort of paté.

88 Checones in Critone

Take checones and make hom clene, and chop hom on quarters, and sethe hom, and when thai byn half sothen take hom up and pylle of the skynne, and frie hom in faire grese and dress hom up, and cast thereon pouder of gynger ande sugur; then take iii pounde of almondes, and blaunche hom, and draw up a gode thik mylke with the brothe, and other gode brothe therewith, and do hit in a pot and sethe hit; and put thereto hole clowes, maces and pynes, and let hit boyle altogedur, and in the settynge down do thereto an ounce of pouder of gynger, and medel hit wyth vynegar, and serve hit forthe, and poure the syrip thereon, and cast thereon pouder of gynger and sugur; and a hole chekyn for a lorde.

ARUNDEL

This recipe (elsewhere in English cookery rolls given in a simplified form called Crayton, calling for cumin and omitting mace and cloves), is particularly remarkable in the helpful

statements of quantity: it is specified to be for 'ten messes,' ie, to serve 20 people; and if only a lord is to be served a whole chicken, we can assume that it is a recipe for five chickens (probably). However, difficulties remain: the French recipe, to which this is obviously related (Cretonée) calls for cow's milk, rather than almond milk, and a thickening of breadcrumbs and/or egg yolks. It also omits vinegar, and is vague about spices. But, most noticeably, it also features fresh peas as part of the sauce. We will therefore give two versions of this dish – one without peas in the English fashion, and one with, as prescribed by the Ménagier.

Chickens in Cream Sauce

I the English version, with slight modifications from the French

1 frying chicken, quartered, or 4-6 chicken legs, cut in halves
2 tbsp ground almonds
lard, oil, or butter (or a combination) for frying
2-3 each whole cloves, peppercorns, maces
1/4 tsp each ground ginger, sugar
1 tsp vinegar
2 egg yolks (may be omitted: but in this case, the quantity
  of almonds should be tripled, or supplemented with breadcrumbs)

Parboil the chicken pieces in salted water to barely cover for about 15 minutes. Drain; remove the chicken skin if you wish to follow the recipe exactly, but it is not really necessary if you let the chicken dry thoroughly before proceeding. Brown the chicken in fat or oil. Meanwhile, add one cup of the broth to the almonds and whole spices and let them steep. When chicken is almost done, bring the sauce to a boil, stirring. Beat egg yolks (if used) in a bowl; pour the sauce onto

the yolks, stirring constantly. Return to the fire and stir over low heat for a few minutes to thicken. Then remove chicken to a serving platter; strain the sauce and add sugar, ground ginger, and vinegar, and pour it over the chicken.

II Checones in Critone with Peas

chicken, as above
2 lbs fresh, young peas, shelled (frozen peas are a poor substitute)
2 1/2 cups milk
1/4 cup (ca) breadcrumbs
1/4 tsp each ginger, sugar
pinch saffron
2 egg yolks or one whole egg (if omitted, increase quantity of breadcrumbs)
lard, oil, and/or butter for frying

Proceed to cook the chicken pieces as directed in the first recipe. Meanwhile, parboil the peas in salted water for 5-10 minutes, depending on size and age (skip this step if using frozen peas). While the chicken is frying, steep the bread-crumbs in 1/2 cup of the chicken broth and 1/2 cup milk. When peas have been parboiled, drain them and set aside. Stir the bread sauce over medium heat until it begins to thicken; add the rest of the milk and seasonings, and taste to see whether more salt is needed. Then add the peas and leave to simmer another five to ten minutes (but no more), while the chicken finishes browning.

When the chicken is done, remove to a serving platter. Strain the peas out of the sauce and scatter them over the chicken. Beat the egg or egg yolks (if used) in a bowl and gradually pour on the hot sauce, stirring constantly; return to the heat, stirring constantly, until sufficiently thick – do not allow to boil. Pour over the chicken and peas and serve at once. (This is not a dish to be completed in advance and re-heated.)

(*more*)

1 For the first version, all spices but ginger and pepper may be omitted, and cumin may be added (1/4 tsp is quite enough).

2 For the second type, veal, goose, or duck may be substituted for chicken, and lima beans or other shell beans may be used instead of peas.

89 Blamanger

Take Capons and seeþ hem; þenne take hem up. Take Almands blanched; grynd hem and alay hem up with the same broth. Cast the mylk in a pot. Waisshe rys and do þerto, and lat it seeþ. Þanne take brawn of Capons, teere it small, and do þerto. Take white grece, sugar and salt, and cast þerinne. Lat it seeþ. Þenne messe it forth and florissh it with aneys in confyt rede oþer whyt, and with Almands fryed in oyle, and serue it forth. FC 36

Rice with Capon or Chicken

1 chicken, or meat from a roast capon, cut up
1 cup raw rice
4 oz (1/2 cup) ground blanched almonds
1 tsp each salt and sugar, or to taste
1/4 tsp ginger
1 tbsp chicken fat or butter (or other cooking fat)
optional: 1/8 tsp cardamom
2-4 tbsp halved or sliced almonds, lightly browned
    in a little oil
1/4-1/2 tsp anise seeds

One capon has too much meat for a recipe on this scale, but the leftovers from a roast are fine; the bones can be used to produce the necessary broth. Of course, leftover roast chicken is also possible – if there is enough for the quantity of the dish desired.

Cover chicken or capon bones with a quart or so of salted water and simmer about 1 hour. Cover rice with cold water and leave to soak. Meanwhile, strain broth, skim off fat, and measure 3 cups of broth into a pan. Stir in almonds; cover and leave to steep about 15 minutes. Then drain water from rice and stir it into the almond broth; bring to a simmer, cover, and cook over low heat for about 15 minutes. Remove skin and bones from the chicken or capon, and cut the meat into small (ca 1-2 inch square) pieces. Stir into the rice along with butter or fat and remaining seasonings. Recover and leave to cook over low heat for 5-10 minutes, or put in a moderate oven for the same amount of time. If dish is to be reheated, undercook, and leave a little on the moist side – add more broth before reheating, if it seems dry. Serve in the casserole in which it was cooked, or mounded on a serving platter, or unmolded; garnish with the sautéed almonds and anise seed.

VARIATIONS

1 Some recipes call for other spices, such as cinnamon; at least one calls for saffron, which is pleasant here but probably inappropriate (a 'blancmanger' does not suggest the colour yellow).

2 Liver and/or giblets of the poultry may be added.

3 A later variant substitutes cream, eggs, and breadcrumbs for rice and broth, moving closer to the dish we know by this name today. Anyone who wishes to try this is reminded that almonds are still essential.

4 See also Blamanger of Fysshe (58).

90 Hoggepot

Take Gees and smyte hem on pecys. Cast hem in a Pot; do þerto half wyne and half water; and do þerto a gode quantite of Oynons and erbest. Set it ouer þe fyre and couer it fast. Make a layor of brede and blode and lay it þerwith. Do þerto powder fort and serue it forth. FC 31

The earliest version of this recipe calls for chicken, rather than goose, and, like many later versions, calls for the poultry to be browned before it is stewed. The following version combines features of several recipes of the period (mostly 14th century), some of which may sound odd – but the result is a really delicious dish.

Hodgepodge of Goose, Duck, or Chicken

1 goose, or 2 ducks, or 2 chickens, cut into pieces
2 cups each beef stock and red wine
4 medium onions, minced
2 tbsp minced parsley
2 tsp each (less if dried) minced sage, thyme, and savory
1/4 tsp each pepper, ginger, and cinnamon, ground (or mixed) with 1 tbsp lemon juice or cider (or wine) vinegar
1 tsp salt
4 slices bread, preferably whole wheat (ca 1 cup crumbs), lightly toasted

First brown the pieces of poultry. Chicken is best browned in a frying pan with a little oil or fat, but goose or duck is very fat in itself and it may be better to brown it, turning frequently, under a broiler, or in a hot oven. Reserve the liver or livers for a later stage: do not brown them. Fry the onions gently in some of the fat (or drippings) when the poultry is brown, but do not let the onions brown. Put poultry pieces

and onions in a dutch oven or other suitable covered pot or casserole; add stock, wine, and herbs; bring to a boil. Turn down the heat, cover tightly, and simmer (or bake in a 325° oven) for about an hour. Toward the end of this time, put the toasted bread (torn up or in crumbs) into a blender jar, bowl, or large mortar, along with uncooked poultry liver or livers and a few spoonfuls of the cooking sauce. With a duck or a goose, you will first have to skim excess fat off the sauce. Let bread soak for a few minutes, then blend, grind, or press through a strainer. Stir this thick paste back into the (degreased) sauce in the pot, along with the spice paste and salt; cook, stirring, for a few more minutes before serving.

VARIATIONS

1 Spices called for elsewhere include cumin, cloves, and mace; any of these may be substituted or added, but do not overdo it. This should not taste spicy.

2 Ale or beer may be substituted for the wine and stock; this will, of course, considerably modify the taste.

3 Since roasting was the usual way of pre-browning poultry, this is an excellent way to use up leftover roast goose, which will already have rendered its excess fat in the roasting and will thus be easier to handle than uncooked or partially cooked goose. Simply decrease all other ingredients in proportion to the amount of meat available, and cut the cooking time by about half.

91 Stwed Beeff

Take faire Ribbes of ffresh beef, And (if thou wilt) roste hit til hit be nygh ynowe; then put hit in a faire possenet; caste þer=to parcely and oynons mynced, reysons of corauns, powder peper, canel, clowes, saundres, safferon, and salt; then caste there=to wyn and a litull vynegre; sette a lyd on þe potte and lete hit boile sokingly on a faire charcole til hit be ynogh; þen lay þe fflessh in disshes, and þe sirippe there=uppon, And serve it forth. HARL 4016

Braised Beef Ribs

1 1/2 to 2 lbs boneless ribs of beef for braising, or about
   1 lb more of meat with the bone in
2-3 onions, minced
2 tbsp parsley, minced
2 tbsp currants
1/2 tsp cinnamon
1/4 tsp each pepper, allspice
1 tsp salt
optional: scant pinch of saffron
1 1/2 cups red wine
2 tsp vinegar (preferably wine vinegar)

Brown the beef by roasting it for about 30 minutes in an open pan in a hot oven, or brown it in a little cooking fat in a frying pan. Then put it in a stew-pot or casserole with all other ingredients. Cover and cook over low heat for about 45 minutes; or cook in a 325° oven for the same amount of time.

VARIATION
To cook in a clay baker, cook the beef by itself for about 45 minutes before adding other ingredients; cut the amount of wine by one half.

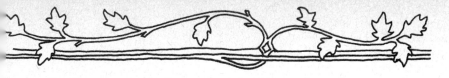

92 A Drye Stewe for Beeff

Take a fair urthen pot, and lay hit well with splentes in the bothum that the flessh neight hit not; then take rybbes of beef or faire leches, and couche hom aboue the splentes, and do therto onyons mynced, and clowes, and maces, and pouder of pepur and wyn, and stop hit well that no eyre goo oute, and sethe hit wyth esy fyre. ARUNDEL

This is an ideal dish to prepare in an unglazed clay baker, but it may also be done in another kind of covered casserole or roaster, using a rack (or improvised splints, as the 15th century recipe prescribes) to keep the beef from touching the bottom of the pot. If you cannot use an unglazed baker, however, you should brown the meat before proceeding with the recipe.

Pot Roast of Beef

a pot roast of beef, or some shortribs – ca 3 lbs
  (chuck is good)
1-2 onions, minced
ca 1/2 tsp each whole cloves, peppercorns, and whole mace
  (or a much smaller quantity of ground cloves, pepper,
  and mace)
1/2 cup red wine

Put the beef in the pot (on rack or splints if the pot does not have a ridged bottom, especially if it is not an unglazed baker) and scatter the onions and spices over it. Then pour over the red wine, close the pot tightly, and roast: about two hours at 325°, or follow whatever procedure you usually use for a pot roast of this size. (With an unglazed baker, many people prefer to bring the temperature nearer to 475°, cutting the cooking time somewhat.) To serve, put the beef on a serving platter and strain the pot juices over it. Thicken the juices if you wish. adding salt to taste.

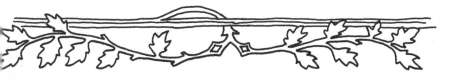

93 Befe in Sirup

Take befe and sklice hit fayre and thynne,
Of þo luddock with owte or ellis with in;
Take mynsud onyouns, and powder also
Of peper, and suet and befe þerto
And cast þeron, rolle hit wele,
Enbroche hit overtwert, so have þou cele;
And rost hit browne as I þe kenne,
And take brothe of fresshe flesshe þenne,
And alye hit with bred er þou more do,
And mynsud onyons þou cast þer to,
With powder of peper and clowes in fere;
Boyle alle togeder, as I þe lere,
Þenne boylyd blode take þou shalle;
Strene hit þorowghe clothe, colour hit withalle;
Þenne take þy rost, and sklyce hit clene
In þe lengthe of a fynger; boyle hit by dene
In the same sewe; serve hit þou may
In a disshe togedur I say. LCC

Braised Stuffed Beef

ca 2 lbs round or rump steak (preferably in one piece)
2 medium onions, peeled and finely minced
ca 4 tbsp beef suet (use fat cut from the outer edge of the
 steak)
1/2 tsp ground black pepper
2 cups beef broth, stock, or boullion
1/4-1/2 cup breadcrumbs (whole wheat bread is appropriate)
pinch ground cloves
1 tsp meat glaze or commercial gravy colouring
 (substituting for blood, which was used for its colour)

Chop the suet and mix with half of the onions and pepper;

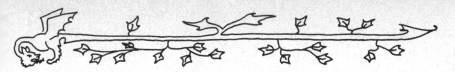

spread this mixture on the steak, roll it up, and fasten shut with skewers or string. Grill (in a broiler or on a spit) until brown. Meanwhile boil remaining ingredients, stirring until thick; strain. Slice the roasted beef and arrange neatly on a fireproof dish suitable for serving; pour the sauce over. Simmer for about five minutes, then serve.

94 Brawn en Peuerade

Take myghty brothe of Beef or of Capoun, an þenne take clene Freyssshe Brawn, an seþe it, but not y=now; An ȝif it be Freyssshe Brawn, roste it, but not I=now, an þan leche it in pecys an caste it to þe brothe. An þanne take hoole Oynonys, & pylle hem, and þanne take Vynagre þer=to, þen take Clowys, Maces, an powder Peppr, and caste þer=to and Canelle, and sette it on þe fyre, and draw yt þorw a straynoure, and caste þer=to, and a lytil Saunderys, and sette it on þe fyre, an let boyle tylle þe Oynonys an þe Brawn ben eyune soþyn, an nowt to moche; þan take lykoure y=mad of Bred an Vinegre an Wyne, an sesyn it vp an caste þer=to Saffroun to make þe coloure bryth, an Salt, and serue it forth. HARL 279.32

Pork in Pepper Sauce

3 lbs boneless pork tenderloin or 4 lbs of another lean, tender pork (not small chunks)
3 tsp wine vinegar
3 tbsp red wine
2 cups beef broth or stock (1 if using a clay baker)
24 very small onions (ca 1 inch) or fewer slightly larger ones, peeled

(*more*)

1/2 tsp each mace, freshly ground black pepper
1/8 tsp cinnamon
pinch ground cloves
optional: pinch saffron, sandalwood spice
1 tsp salt, or more
1/4 cup breadcrumbs or 1-2 slices bread, soaked in the wine

Brown the meat in a frying pan, unless you are using a clay baker or leftover roast pork. Put pork, onions, salt, spices, and 1 tsp of the vinegar into a clay baker or casserole. Pour the stock over and put in oven, preheated to 350° (if using clay baker, adjust accordingly). Cover tightly. Cook 1 1/4–2 hours, depending on type of cooker and temperature; remove meat to a serving platter and slice neatly. Keep warm while making sauce.

Strain cooking juices into a bowl, reserving onions. Blend breadcrumbs or soaked bread with wine and 2 tsp vinegar until very smooth; beat in cooking juices and stir in a saucepan with the reserved onions until sauce is hot, smooth, and thick; then pour over the meat on its platter and serve.

This can also be prepared on top of the stove, but since pork takes long cooking the oven method is preferable – and the turned-off oven provides a place to keep the meat warm while the sauce is prepared.

95 Tartlett

Take pork ysode and grynde it small with safron, medle it with ayren and raisons of coraunce and powdor fort and salt; and make a foile of dowh₃ and close the fars þerinne. Cast þe Tartlet in a Panne with faire water boillyng and salt; take of the clene Flessh withoute ayren and boile it in gode broth; cast þerto powdor douce and salt, and messe the tartlet in the dissh and helde the sewe þeronne. FC 50

Boiled Meat Dumplings in Broth

2 cups ground cooked pork
1/4 cup currants
1/4 tsp salt
pinch to 1/4 tsp of any or all of: ground cloves, ginger,
  pepper, cubebs, galingale (for powder fort)
1 egg
2 cups broth (meat or chicken)
pinch to 1/4 tsp of any or all of: cinnamon, cardamom,
  coriander, mace (for powdor douce)

In a small bowl mix one cup of ground cooked pork, the currants, salt, spices fort, and egg. Either make a paste of flour
and water/egg (use a noodle recipe) and roll it very thin, or
buy commercially made sheets of dough for eggrolls or won-
tons. Cut into 2 inch squares. Moisten the edge of the paste
with beaten egg or water, place a spoonful of the meat mixture in the middle, and fold over so the edges meet (to make
a triangle shape). Press edges together. Boil the tartlets in
salted water until the paste is cooked.

Add the other cup of ground cooked pork to the broth,
with douce spices and salt. Heat the mixture, add the tartlets, and serve.

VARIATION
Like Won Tons, which they closely resemble, these dump-
lings may be fried rather than boiled.

96 Monchelet

Take Veel oþer Moton and smite it to gobetts; seeþ it in gode broth. Cast þerto erbes yhewe, gode wyne, and a quan=tite of Oynons, mynced. Powdor fort and Safron; and alye it with ayren and verjious: but lat not seeþ after. FC 16

This dish bears some resemblance to a modern Blanquette de Veau, but has a distinctive character of its own a bit different from any modern recipe. Since the primary purpose of the saffron appears to be colouring, we advise that this be omitted, or a drop of food colouring substituted.

A Veal or Lamb Stew

1 1/2 to 2 lbs veal stewing meat
1 1/2 to 2 cups chicken broth
1 cup white wine
2 medium onions, minced
1 tbsp minced parsley
1/2 to 1 tsp each (depending on whether fresh or dried
  herbs are used) thyme, rosemary, savory
1/4 tsp each ground ginger and coriander
salt to taste (depending on how well salted broth is)
1 egg
juice of 1/2 lemon (ca 2 tbsp; or use cider vinegar)
optional: pinch of saffron

Cut veal into pieces – about 2 inches square is ideal – and put in a cooking pot, preferably enamelled. Add onions, herbs, and spices, and cover with wine and broth. Simmer for about 45 minutes, covered. Beat egg together with lemon juice or vinegar. Pour a little of the hot (but not boiling) sauce into the egg and lemon mixture, stirring; then add this to the con-tents of the saucepan, off the heat. Stir off the heat or over very low heat to thicken; do not allow to boil after adding egg.

A similar dish, called Corat, calls for loin of veal, pork, or lamb (actually 'Noumbles,' but this may mean kidneys, or other organ meats), parboiled before it is cut up and put in broth to finish cooking. Otherwise, the recipe is identical.

97 Hericot de Mouton

Cut it up into little pieces, then put it to parboil in a first water. Then fry it in fresh lard; fry it with onions minced small, and add beef boullion, and put with it maces, parsley, hyssop, and sage; boil it together. MP

Later English recipes invariably call for turnips in a stew called Haricot. They may also have been a common ingredient earlier: early recipes are so few and far between that one cannot tell. By all means add turnips, if you like, to this recipe. We skip the parboiling as unnecessary for fresh young lamb: if you are using mutton, however, parboil it.

Lamb or Mutton Stew

3 lbs lamb (or mutton) stewing meat, cut into chunks
4 onions (ca), minced
lard, butter, or other cooking fat for browning (ca 1 tbsp)
2 cups beef stock, boullion, or other meat broth
1-2 tbsp fresh parsley, chopped
1 tsp salt (or to taste)
1/2 tsp each minced sage and mint (we did not find dried
    hyssop at all flavourful, and prefer to substitute mint,
    which is of the same family; if you grow hyssop, you may
    wish to try it)
1/4 tsp ground mace

Remove excess fat and bones from lamb. Brown over medium heat in a frying pan with fat, adding the minced onions after meat begins to brown. When meat and onions are both sufficiently brown, put in a pot or casserole with herbs, stock, mace, and salt; simmer for about an hour, or cook covered in a medium oven. If the sauce appears to be too thin, a thickening may be used (for example, cornstarch), but it should boil down to a good consistency.

98 Stwed Mutton

Take faire Mutton that hath ben roste, or elles Capons, or suche oþer flessh, and mynce it faire; put hit into a possenet or elles betwen ii. siluer disshes; caste thereto faire parcely, And oynons small mynced; then caste there=to wyn, and a litull vynegre or vergeous, pouder of peper, Canel, salt and saffron, and lete it stue on þe faire coles, And þen serue hit forthe; if he haue no wyne ne vynegre, take Ale, Mustard, and A quantite of vergeous, and do þis in þe stede of vyne or vinegre. HARL 4016

Reheated Lamb in Wine Sauce

2-3 cups leftover roast lamb or mutton, cut into fairly small
   chunks
2-3 onions, minced
ca 1/4 cup parsley, minced
1 tsp salt
1/4 tsp each pepper and cinnamon
optional: pinch of ground saffron
4 tsp vinegar or lemon juice
1 cup wine (preferably red)

Heat all ingredients together in a suitable pan, or in a shallow heatproof serving dish; the mixture should be simmered for at least 10 minutes to evaporate the alcohol sufficiently and cook the onions, but no more than 25 minutes, or the parsley will become overcooked. If a thickening is desired, stir in some cornstarch dissolved in cold water and stir a few minutes more.

VARIATIONS

1 Other roasted meats, such as chicken, may be substituted for the lamb. Some meats will, of course, do better with red wine – beef, for example; while white may be used with others.

2 Ale or beer may be substituted for wine. If mustard is added to this version, omit the cinnamon.

99 Egurdouce

Take Conynges or Kydde and smyte hem on pecys rawe, and frye hem in white grece. Take raysons of Corance and fry hem; take opnons, parboile hem and hew hem small and fry hem. Take rede wine, sugar, with powdor of peper, of gynger, of canel; salt; and cast þerto; and lat it seeþ with a gode quantite of white grece; and serue it forth. FC 21

'Egurdouce' (other spellings of the world include Egredouncye) means 'sweet-and-sour,' derived from French Aigredoux; oddly, about half the recipes omit one or the other essential aspect. This recipe omits the sour part; at least two others include vinegar but forget sugar. Etymology plus the few recipes that do include both vinegar and sugar suggest we should remedy the omission. Lamb is suggested as a reasonable substitute for kid, and breadcrumbs added as a thickener, as in most other recipes for the dish.

Sweet and Sour Lamb

2-3 lbs lamb stew meat, cut up in chunks (ca 2 inch)
butter or other cooking fat (about 2 tbsp)
1/4 cup currants
2-3 onions
1 1/2 cups red wine
1/2 cup vinegar
1/2 cup sugar
1/2 tsp each ginger and cinnamon
1/4 tsp pepper
1 tsp salt (or more: to taste)
ca 2 tbsp breadcrumbs

Melt butter or fat in a frying pan or dutch oven and brown the pieces of lamb in it; when lamb is almost brown enough, add currants. Meanwhile, cover onions with cold water and bring to a boil, then drain off the water and chop the onions; add them to the lamb and currants and fry a few minutes more. Then add wine, vinegar, sugar, and seasonings; cover, and let simmer for about 45 minutes. Thicken with the breadcrumbs, mixed to a paste with a few spoonfuls of the sauce first.

VARIATIONS
1 Use rabbit, pork, beef, or chicken instead of the lamb.
2 Add parsley, sage, and/or other herbs.
3 Add ground cloves, mace, and/or sandalwood spice.
4 Add a pinch of saffron.
5 Parboil the meat before browning; or brown the meat by broiling or roasting it; then chop and put in the broth, thus eliminating the fat from the recipe.

100 Gruelle A-forsydde

Take otemele an grynd it smal, an sethe it wyl, an porke
þer=ynne, an pulle of þe swerde an pyke owt þe bonys, an
þan hewe it, an grynd it smal in a morter; þan neme þin
grwel and do þer=to; þan strayne it þorw a straynour, and
put it in a potte an sethe it a lytel, an salt it euene; an
colour it wyth saffroun, an serue forth rennyng. HARL 279.7

Another recipe for this dish calls for beef rather than pork,
and suggests seasoning with sage and parsley rather than saffron. The latter seasoning is just as good with pork, and
subtly transforms this admittedly simple and homely concoc-
tion. It seems an especially useful dish for using up the last
bit of a roast: therefore the directions assume a piece of at
least partly cooked meat.

Meat Porridge

Cooked piece of beef or pork, preferably with bone in,
    but enough meat on the bones to yield about 2 cups of
    chopped meat
5 cups water
one onion, peeled and chopped
ca 2 tbsp minced parsley
2-3 sage leaves, or about 1/4 tsp dried sage
1 tsp salt (or more, to taste)
1 1/2 cups quick-cooking oatmeal

Put onion and meat in a pan with the water and salt; simmer
for about 15 minutes. Then remove meat; discard bone and
any skin. Chop the meat finely, or put it through a grinder
(or in a blender for a few seconds, with some of the broth).
Then mix together in the pan meat, oatmeal, herbs, and
broth, and bring to a boil. Boil, stirring, for about 3 minutes,
then cover and leave, off the heat, for about five minutes before serving.

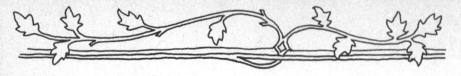

101 Civey of Coney

To mak cony or malard in cevy tak cony henne or malard
and rost them till they be almost enoughe or else chope them
and fry them in freche grece and fry onyons mynced and put
them in a pot and cast ther to freche brothe and half wyne
clowes maces pouder of guinger and pepper and draw it with
benygar and when it is boiled cast ther to thy licour and
pouder of guingere and benygar and sesson it and serue
it. N

This recipe omits, no doubt through someone's inadvertence,
an important ingredient invariably called for elsewhere: a
bread thickening, generally made with toasted bread.

Rabbit Stewed with Onions

1 rabbit, whole or cut into pieces
3-4 onions, sliced or chopped (1 1/2 to 2 cups chopped onion)
ca 2 tbsp cooking fat .
1 cup each chicken or meat broth, red wine
1/4 tsp each ginger, pepper (ginger may be slightly increased)
1/8 tsp mace; pinch of clove
1/2 tsp salt, or to taste (this depends on the broth)
2 slices bread (preferably wholewheat), toasted
1 tbsp wine vinegar

Roast the rabbit until brown, then cut it up, or start by
browning pieces of rabbit in the fat. In either case, when
pieces are brown, add onions to pan and cook together in fat
until onions are soft. Meanwhile, soak the toast in broth.
Then mash the toast through a strainer, or blend it with the
broth in a blender. Add this bread paste to the rabbit and
onions, along with the rest of the broth and wine, vinegar,
and all seasonings. Let the meat stew in this sauce until done,

or at least long enough for the flavours to blend, if the rabbit is already roasted: this will take at least half an hour for rabbit that has only been browned in fat, and 10-15 minutes for roasted rabbit, but overcooking will not hurt this stew.

VARIATIONS

1 As the original recipe indicates, duck or chicken – among other meats – may be cooked the same way.

2 Some recipes substitute ale for wine, or use meat broth alone; we think the dish less interesting if only broth is used, but certainly ale or beer is a variant many may prefer.

3 Other spices sometimes called for include cinnamon and nutmeg. If you wish to add either one, do not overdo it: try adding 1/8 tsp of either or both. The most important seasoning is clearly the ginger (note that the whole spice mixture is simply referred to as 'ginger' the second time it is mentioned in the original recipe above); thus it may be appropriate to increase the amount of ginger to 1/2 tsp. Other seasonings sometimes called for are parsley and saffron. We do not see the point of saffron here, but think it a nice touch to sprinkle the stew with some minced parsley just before serving.

102 Garbage

Take fayre garbagys of chykonys, as þe hed, þe fete, þe lyuerys, an þe gysowrys; wasshe hem clene, an caste hem in a fayre potte, and caste þer=to freyssþe brothe of Beef or ellys of moton, an let it boyle; an a=lye it wyth brede, an ley on Pepir an Safroun, Maces, Clowyse, an a lytil verious an salt, an serue forth in þe maner as a Sewe.

HARL 279.17

Even the most enthusiastic of medievalists may feel qualms about serving or eating stewed chicken heads, so be selective about which 'garbage' you use. A dish made of livers alone is apt to be highest in general appeal, but hearts and gizzards

can also be used successfully. The recipe below calls for a mixture of these. Anyone who prefers to eliminate either the livers or the other giblets may adapt it accordingly.

Giblets

1 lb giblets (chicken hearts and gizzards)
1 lb chicken livers
1 cup (ca) brown stock, broth, or beef boullion
1 tsp salt
1/4 to 1/2 cup breadcrumbs
1/4 tsp each ground pepper, saffron (optional), and mace
1/8 tsp ground cloves
1 tsp verjuice (use cider vinegar or lemon juice)
1/2 tsp ground sage
2 tbsp chopped parsley

Put the gizzards and hearts in a saucepan with the stock and bring to a boil; simmer for 25-30 minutes. Then add livers, and simmer for another 5 minutes. Now stir in all seasonings (except the verjuice) and the breadcrumbs; stir until sauce seems well thickened. Add verjuice just before serving.

The sauce will be smoother if you can blend it in a blender, of course. Or you may use a thickener other than bread: flour, cornstarch, etc, observing the proper procedures for the thickener of your choice.

103 Noumbles

Take noumbles of Deer oþer of oþer beest; parboile hem; kerf hem to dyce. Take þe self broth or better; take brede and grynde with þe broth, and temper it up with a gode quantite of vynegar and wyne. Take þe oynons and par=

boyle þem, anð mynce þem smale anð ðo þer=to. Color it
with bloðe anð ðo þer=to powðor fort anð ſalt, anð boyle it
wele, anð ſerue it forth. FC 13

'Noumbles' is a confusing term because it is sometimes a
word for loin meat and sometimes for organ meats. In refer-
ence to deer, however, it can be assumed that organ meats are
intended – nor does this sort of recipe sound at all the normal
way of cooking a loin, which would, of course, be roasted.
We have assumed the kidney to be the best meat for the recipe, but liver or heart, or a combination of organ meats,
could be substituted.

Kidney Stew

2 beef kidneys (ca 1 1/2-2 lbs)
3/4 cup beef broth or stock
1/4 cup breadcrumbs
2 tbsp vinegar
1/4 cup red wine
2-3 onions, peeled
1/4 tsp each ginger, mace, and pepper
1/2 tsp salt (or to taste)

Cover the kidneys with cold, salted water and bring to a boil;
then pour off the water (or save it for broth, if you have no
beef stock). Chop the kidneys into pieces about one inch
square, or a little more. Beat the breadcrumbs into the broth
(starting by moistening with just a tablespoon or two) and
stir in the wine and vinegar.

Meanwhile, parboil onions in salted water for about five
minutes. Drain, and chop the onions. Add them along with
seasonings and chopped kidneys to the sauce and bring to a
simmer; cover and cook gently for 25-30 minutes.

(more)

Substitute ale or beer for the wine and vinegar, using about half ale and half broth; season with 1/4 tsp pepper. Onions may be omitted.

104 A Tile of Meat

Take cooked crayfish and remove the meat from the tails; the rest, shells and carcase, should be ground for a very long time. Then take unpeeled almonds and have them shelled and washed in hot water like peas, then ground with the shells spoken of above, and with them grind bread browned on the grill. Then you should have capons, chickens, and pullets, broken into quarters raw, or veal broken into portions, cooked; and with the broth in which they are cooked moisten and dilute what you have ground and then put it through a strainer. Then grind what is left in the strainer again and strain again. Add ginger, cinnamon, clove, and long pepper, moistened with verjuice without vinegar, and boil all this together. Now let your meat be cooked in lard in gobbets or quarters, and serve it forth in bowls, and pour the sauce over it and on the sauce, in each bowl, set four or five crayfish tails, with powdered sugar over all. MP

This dish, a real *pièce de résistance*, should not be attempted without a blender, or, at the very least, a large mortar and pestle. With a blender it is much easier and faster, but still takes some time and patience. It is worth it. The quantity given here is for a main course for four people; to serve six or more (including presentation as one of several dishes to be sampled at a feast), cut the chicken into smaller pieces, but try to arrange the pieces into the same sort of patterned effect, which is no doubt the source of the name 'tile' here.

Chicken and Shellfish in Shellfish Sauce

1 frying chicken, cut into quarters
2-3 tbsp cooking fat
4 or 8 (depending on size) crayfish, lobster tails, or scampi;
in a pinch, use shrimp (the largest you can find; at least
half a pound)
1/4 cup blanched almonds (they need not be ground in
advance)
1-2 slices (depending on size) white bread, toasted
2 cups chicken broth or stock (use neck and giblets of
chicken to make some, if you have none on hand)
1 tsp lemon juice or cider vinegar
1/8 tsp ground ginger
pinch each cinnamon, clove, pepper
salt to taste

Cover the shellfish with wine and water plus a little salt and
cook for about five minutes, depending on the size of the
shellfish. Drain (but reserve broth for part of the stock) and
shell, keeping crayfish, scampi, tails, or shrimp whole, and reserving shells and all debris (such as roe). Soak the toasted
bread in a little broth. Dry the shells (and etc, if any) with
paper towelling and put through a meat grinder or chop as
finely as possible. Then put the shells in a blender (or mortar)
with the almonds, bread, and enough broth to cover and
blend until it is very finely pulverized and as smooth as possible. Rub through a strainer; then return what is left in the
strainer to the blender, add a bit more broth, and repeat the
process. Put the strained mixture in a saucepan and stir in
any remaining broth. Add the spices, dissolved in the lemon
juice or vinegar, and bring to a boil. Stir for about five minutes or until slightly thickened; then cover and put aside.

Sauté the chicken pieces in fat, turning to brown both
sides; this will take about 45 minutes, but if you wish to do
it in advance, undercook and reheat in a covered casserole at
the last minutes. (We do not think it necessary to parboil
chicken first, as it was in the 14th century: but you may if

you wish. It does tend to make it harder to brown the chicken, however, unless you let the chicken cool and dry out after it has been parboiled.)

When you are ready to serve the dish, reheat the shellfish gently in a little bit of the sauce, while also reheating the rest of the sauce (and, if necessary, the chicken). Arrange the chicken in a quartered circle on a fairly deep platter; pour the sauce over it. Then arrange the shellfish between the pieces of chicken (but on top) so that the whole dish will have an appropriate tile-like pattern, and serve.

Desserts

Most – although by no means all – medieval feasts ended with a sweet course; though the word 'dessert' was not common, it originated in this period and the concept was commonplace enough. Most such last courses consisted of simple offerings such as fruits (some of which, however, were also eaten as a first course, as modern diners eat melons or fruit cup), nuts, cheeses, candied spices (such as preserved, candied ginger), wafers, and sweet spiced wines. But there are many other medieval dishes which we would think of as desserts today.

105 Strawberyes with Creme Bastard

Take þe whyte of Eyroun a grete hepe, & putte it on a panne ful of Mylke, & let yt boyle; þen sesyn it so with Salt an hony a lytel; þen lat hit kele, & draw it þorw a straynoure, an take fayre Cowe mylke an draw yt with-all, & seson it with Sugre; & loke þat it be poynant & doucet: & serue it forth for a potage, or for a gode Bakyn mete, wheder þat þou wolt. HARL 279.151

This is a recipe for custard, but made in quite the opposite way from the usual modern sauce in that whites, instead of yolks, are used.

Strawberries with White Custard Sauce

1 qt strawberries, washed, hulled, and sprinkled with
  ca 1 tbsp sugar
2 egg whites
1 cup plus 2 tsp milk
2 tbsp honey
pinch salt
2 tsp sugar

Put egg whites in a sauce pan with 1 cup of the milk, and stir over medium heat as it comes to a boil. Let it simmer for about 5 minutes, stirring; then add the honey and salt. After simmering for another minute or two, remove from heat and strain or blend in a blender, adding remaining milk and sugar. Pour into a pitcher or serving dish and chill; it will thicken as it chills.

Serve over washed, hulled, slightly sweetened strawberries.

106 Wardonys in Syrpp

𝕿ake wardonys, an caste on a potte, and boyle hem till þey ben tender; þan take hem vp and pare hem, and kytte hem in to pecys; take y=now of powder of canel, a good quantyte, an caste it on red wyne, an draw it þorw a strapnour; caste sugre þer=to, and put it in an erþen pot, and let it boyle: an þanne caste þe perys þer=to, an let boyle to=gederys, an whan þey haue boyle a whyle, take pouder of gyngere and caste þer=to an a lytil venegre, an a lytil safron; an loke þat it be poynaunt an dowcet. HARL 279.10

Another early recipe is reported to include cloves, and to call for longer, slower cooking. We will thus offer alternative instructions in this matter.

Pears in Wine Syrup

2 lbs firm, ripe, unblemished pears
2 cups red wine (or, if preferred, 1 cup wine and 1 cup water)
1/2 cup sugar
1 tsp cinnamon
1/4 tsp ginger
optional spices: 6-8 whole cloves; pinch of saffron
1 tbsp lemon juice (or do as later cooks did and use a strip
    of lemon or orange peel; or use vinegar)

Parboil the pears in a large pot of water for about 5 minutes; remove and peel. Pears will look most attractive if left whole, but if you cut them up, cut lengthwise into halves or quarters, retaining stems, if possible, but removing stem lines and cores. Mix cinnamon and red wine (or wine and water) and strain the mixture into a pan (enamelled, if pears are to be cooked in same vessel). Add sugar and stir over heat until the sugar is dissolved. Then, either:

1 add pears to syrup and poach gently for about 10 minutes, keeping the syrup just below the simmering point to keep the pears from falling apart. Add ginger, lemon juice (or vinegar or peel), and saffron and/or cloves, if desired, toward the end of the cooking period. Let pears cool in the syrup. Or:

2 Put pears in an enamelled or earthenware casserole, with remaining ingredients. Pour sugar syrup over them; cover casserole and bake in a 250° oven for about 5 hours, turning pears from time to time, or cook covered on the stove over very low heat 6-8 hours. Remove pears to dish in which they will be served. If the quantity of syrup is excessive, boil it down a bit to thicken it. Pour syrup over pears and store in a cool place, or in refrigerator, where they will keep well for several days. Serve them in their syrup.

107 Strawberye

Take Strawberys, & waysshe hem in tyme of ȝere in gode red wyne; þan strayne þorwe a cloþe, & do hem in a potte with gode Almaunde mylke, a-lye it with Amyndoun oþer with þe flowre of Rys, & make it chargeaunt and lat it boyle, and do þer-in Roysonys of coraunce, Safroun, Pepir, Sugre grete plente, pouder Gyngere, Canel, Galyngale; poynte it with Vynegre, & a lytil whyte grece put þer-to; coloure it with Alkenade, & droppe it abowte, plante it with þe graynys of Pome=garnad, & þan serue it forth.

HARL 279.123

This recipe has been much maligned. Mead was among the writers horrified at the idea of so treating strawberries. But if one keeps a delicate touch with the spices (as most medieval cooks must have had to, considering their expense), the result is not unlike a modern strawberry mousse: it is, in fact, delicious.

Strawberry Pudding

1 pt fresh strawberries (if you must use the frozen kind,
    the juice should be substituted for some of the liquid in
    the recipe)
1/4-1/2 cup red wine
2 oz (1/4 cup) ground almonds
2 tbsp rice flour or cornstarch
1/3 cup sugar
1 1/4 cup water
pinch each pepper, ginger, cinnamon, salt
2 tbsp dried currants
1 tbsp lard or butter
2 tsp wine vinegar (or lemon juice)

Hull and pick over the strawberries, cutting out any bad places. Put in a bowl and pour the wine over them. Mix gently with your hand or a wood or plastic spoon; then pour off and discard the wine. Force strawberries through a sieve into a pot, and blend in remaining ingredients – or put them in a blender and blend everything together – except for the fat, vinegar, and currants. Bring mixture to a boil over medium heat, stirring constantly; let it boil for about two minutes to thicken, then remove at once and stir in, first, the fat, then the vinegar and currants. Pour into a large serving dish or individual serving dishes, and allow to cool. Chill before serving.

If you are as much of a perfectionist as the 15th century cook from whom this recipe comes apparently was, you may

beef up the colouring with red vegetable dye and/or garnish the pudding with pomegranate seeds, but it really is not necessary.

VARIATION

Turnesole, blackberry pudding, is made much the same way. Use blackberries instead of strawberries and omit spices, currants, lard, and vinegar. This is good hot, but some may wish to strain out the seeds at some point.

108 Ioncate with Hurtilberyes

Strawberie & hurtilberyes with the cold Ioncate

are mentioned in John Russell's *Boke of Nurture*. Russell lists Ioncate in conjunction with 'Milke, crayme, and cruddes.' He does not tell us how to make it, but another authority reports it to be 'a certaine spoone-meat made of creame, Rosewater, and Sugar,' and it is elsewhere said to be a species of cream cheese. The etymology of the word is generally accounted to derive from reed baskets in which this 'cream cheese' was drained of its whey. Later cookbooks – for example, the nineteenth-century editions of *Fanny Farmer* – invariably give a recipe for milk sweetened and thickened with rennet, which is, of course, what we call junket today. Rennet is a basic ingredient of both cheese and modern junkets. The question, then, is not what went into a medieval junket – that is clear enough; but whether it was set and served in the same dish, after one cooking procedure, as is the case with junkets today, or made into a cheese and drained. The latter seems more likely in the earlier period, but it is a great deal more trouble. We therefore prefer a recipe made as today's junket is made – but with medieval ingredients. Those who wish to try a variety more like cream cheese should consult the directions for cottage cheese which come with packets of plain rennet tablets, and adapt the procedure accordingly.

Junket with Blueberries

2 cups light cream

2 tsp rosewater (if your usual market does not stock this, try
a specialty store, delicatessen, health food store, or
pharmacy)

2 tbsp sugar

1 tablet plain, unflavoured rennet, dissolved in 1 tbsp
cold water

Blueberries, or, if in season, strawberries; if you must use
frozen berries, blueberries usually have a better texture

If your grocery store does not stock plain rennet tablets,
substitute vanilla junket powder for the rennet, water, and
sugar; but, of course, the flavour will be pronounced (and
anachronistic). If you can get liquid rennet, use the amount
advised for 2 cups of milk.

Mix cream, rosewater, and sugar in a saucepan and heat to
barely lukewarm, stirring occasionally to dissolve sugar. A
candy thermometer is helpful to assure reaching the best temperature, ca 100° F; no higher than 110°, for rennet mixtures
will be spoiled if they boil. Meanwhile, dissolve rennet tablet
in cold water. If cream overheats, allow it to cool before proceeding. Stir dissolved rennet into lukewarm cream as quickly
as possible: it takes only seconds. Pour *at once* into the individual dishes from which it will be eaten – custard cups, sher-
bet glasses, etc. For serving smaller helpings to guests at a
Feast, small stiff foil cases will do. Let it sit undisturbed for
10-15 minutes, then chill. To serve, put sweetened berries on
top.

109 Rede Rose

Take the same [ie, using roses, follow recipe for violets, boiled, pressed, and ground, cooked in milk or almond milk thickened with rice flour and sweetened with sugar], saue a=lye it with þe ȝolkes of eyroun. HARL 279.126

Red Rose Pudding

1 cup rose petals (use red roses that are just beginning to go,
    discarding any really wilted spots, as you would with greens)
2 tbsp rice flour or cornstarch
1/4 tsp salt
2 cups milk
1/4 cup sugar (scant; some may prefer to use only 3 tbsp)
3 egg yolks or one whole egg plus one yolk

Plunge the rose petals into boiling water and boil for about 5 minutes; drain away water and leave to dry on absorbant paper. The best way to dry them thoroughly is to put several layers of paper above and below the petals, then put a heavy weight, such as a cast-iron pan, on top. When petals are reasonably dry, mix the rice flour or starch into a paste with some of the milk. Then put this paste into a blender with the sugar and rose petals. (If you have no blender, you will have to pulverize the petals by some other method, such as grinding in a mortar with the sugar, before proceeding.) Blend, gradually adding the rest of the milk and the salt. Stir this mixture over medium heat until it has the consistency of a thick sauce – about 5 minutes. Remove from heat. Beat egg yolk (or egg and yolk), and then beat in a little of the warm pudding. Stir this back into the rest of the pudding, and stir over very low heat for another 5 minutes, or until very thick. The colour will be a pale violet: you may wish to add a drop or two of red food colouring to make it look rosier. Pour into a bowl or individual dishes and chill before serving.

Violets or hawthorne blossoms may be treated the same way, but the 15th century directions say to omit egg yolks for these flower puddings. It is thus advised that you substitute 2 oz (1/4 cup) ground almonds for the eggs and use one cup each milk and water; the whole pudding can be cooked in one step, since there is no need to worry about curdling.

110 Erbowle

𝕿ake bolas and scald hem with wyne and drawe hem with a strynor; do hem in a pot; clarify hony and do þerto, with powdor fort and floer of Rhys. Salt it & florish it with whyte aneys, & serue it forth. FC 95

This fresh fruit pudding is like the modern Scandinavian berry and rhubarb puddings, and not to be confused with the traditional Christmas pudding.

Plum Pudding

1 lb ripe fresh plums
1 cup each red wine, water
1/4 cup clear honey
1/4 cup cornstarch or rice flour, dissolved in 1/4 cup cold
 water
1/2 tsp salt
1/4 tsp cinnamon
1/8 tsp each galingale or ginger, mace
ca 1/2 tsp anise seed

Put plums in a saucepan and cover with wine and water. Bring to a boil and simmer for about 5 minutes. Remove plums; peel them and discard pits. Press plums through a

strainer or blend in a blender; add honey and all spices (except anise) to the puréed plums, and stir this mixture back into the cooking liquid in the saucepan. Stir in the dissolved starch carefully: it must be thoroughly blended for about 5 minutes; it should be quite thick. If there are lumps, restrain or blend. Pour into a serving bowl; cool; then chill. Scatter anise seeds on top when the pudding is well set. It is good served with whipped cream or vanilla ice cream, if you do not object to a non-medieval touch.

111 Pomesmoille

Nym rys & bray hem in a morter, tempre hem up with almande milke, boille hem: nym appelis & kerue hem as small as douste, cast hem yn after ye boillyng, & sugur: colour hit with safron, cast therto goud poudre, & ʒif hit forth. LAUD 553

Apple-Almond Pudding

1/4 cup rice flour (or cornstarch)
1/4 cup ground almonds
2 cups water, milk, or a combination of the two
1 lb cooking apples, pared, cored, and diced (fine)
pinch each ground clove, salt, nutmeg
1/2 cup sugar (less if apples are sweet)
1/2 tsp cinnamon
1/8 tsp ginger
optional: pinch of ground saffron or a drop of yellow
   food colouring

Mix sugar, rice flour, ground almonds, and water and/or milk in a saucepan; stir in apples and bring to a boil over medium heat. Stir and boil for about 5 minutes, or until pudding is

quite thick. Mix all seasonings except nutmeg in a small dish or cup with a spoonful of the pudding, then stir this into the rest of the pudding. When thoroughly blended, pour into a serving dish. Sprinkle nutmeg on top and cool and/or chill. This can be served as it is or, if preferred, with cream.

VARIATION

One recipe adds chopped or slivered almonds ('shere them smale'), which makes a pleasant variation in texture and can be strongly recommended; if desired, add about 1/4 cup finely slivered almonds along with the spices.

112 Chiresepe

Tak Chirpes at the ffest of Seynt John the Baptist and do away the stonys; grynd hem in a morter, and after frot hem wel in a sebe so that the Jus be wel compyn owt; and do than in a pot, and do therein feyr gres or Botor, and bred of wastrel ymincid, and of sugur a god party, and a porcion of wyn; and wan it is wel ysoden and ydressed in Dyschis, stik therein clowis of Gilofre and strew thereon sugur.

AC II.18

Cherry Bread Pudding

2 cups fresh, sour pie cherries, stoned; or 20 oz (2 cans) pie
    cherries, drained, plus the juice of 1/2 lemon
2 cups breadcrumbs
1/3 cup sugar
3/4 cup red wine (or 1/2 cup wine plus 1/4 cup water or
    juice from canned cherries)
1 tbsp butter

The easiest way to make this is with a blender: if you have one, put in all ingredients except butter and blend, then put

in pan, adding butter. If not, mash the cherries and force through a strainer, then mix with other ingredients before proceeding. Cook, stirring constantly, over a medium fire for about five minutes, or until well thickened. Pour into a serving dish, or individual dishes, and let cool – or chill in a refrigerator. Sprinkle with ground cloves (sparingly), if you wish, with or without extra sugar. This is particularly good served with cream – or with Creme Bastarde (105).

VARIATION
After stirring over heat for a moment or two, pour into a greased baking dish and bake in a 350° oven for about 20 minutes. Serve hot or cold.

113 Milkemete

Take faire mylke and floure, and draue hem þorgh a streyn=
our, and sette hem ouer the fire, and lete hem boyle awhile;
And then take hem vppe, and lete hem kele awhile. And þen
take rawe yolkes of eyren and drawe hem thorgh a streyn=
our, and caste thereto a litull salt, And set it ouer the fire til
hit be som=what thik, And lete hit noȝt fully boyle, and
stere it right well euermore. And put it in a dissh al
abrode, And serue it forth for a gode potage in one maner;
And then take Sugur a good quantite, And caste there=to,
and serue it forth. HARL 4016

Milk Custard Pudding

2 cups milk
1/4 cup flour (instant-blending may be safest)
4 egg yolks or two whole eggs
1/8 tsp salt
1/4 cup brown sugar (either light or dark, but demerara,
  if you can get it, is best for this)

Mix the flour to a paste with the milk, gradually adding the rest of the milk – in a blender, if you have one. Bring to a boil in a saucepan, and let it simmer, stirring occasionally, until somewhat thickened. Meanwhile, beat yolks or eggs with the salt. Beat a little of the milk mixture into the eggs, then the rest; return to the pan, and cook over low heat, stirring continually, until well thickened. It is best not to let the mixture boil, but it is less apt to curdle than a normal modern custard because of the flour. Put in a bowl (or individual dishes) and sprinkle the sugar on top. Serve warm or cold. Chilled, it tastes rather like a crème caramel.

114 Rys

Take a porcyoun of Rys, & pyke hem clene, & sethe hem welle, & late hem kele; þen take gode Mylke of Almaundys & do þer-to, & seþe & stere hem wyl; & do þer-to Sugre an hony, & serue forth. HARL 279.86

Rice Pudding with Honey and Almonds

1/2 cup short grain rice
2 1/2 cups milk, water, or a combination
4 oz (1/2 cup) ground almonds blanched
1/4 cup sugar
2 tbsp honey
1 cup boiling water

Cover the rice with milk (or whatever combination you wish here) and bring to a simmer; cook over low heat, very gently, for at least 30 minutes, stirring occasionally and adding more water if it shows signs of drying out. It should be cooked until quite soft. Then remove from heat and put aside to cool, so that any remaining cooking liquid is absorbed.

Meanwhile, put the almonds, sugar, and honey in a pan and cover with boiling water. Stir and allow to steep. When rice has cooled, stir the almond mixture into the rice and put back on the heat; cook, stirring constantly, over medium low heat for about 5 minutes, or until pudding seems quite thick. Remove from heat and pour into serving dish; cool and chill.

The original recipe does not call for any spices. But on the assumption that the medieval cook often reached for powder douce (or something) almost automatically, as we do salt and pepper, it seems permissible to sprinkle the top of the pudding with cinnamon and/or nutmeg.

115 Fygey

𝕿ake Almands blanched; grynde hem and drawe hem up with water and wyne; quarter fygs, hole raisons. Cast þerto powdor gynger and hony clarified; seeþ it wel & salt it, and serue forth. FC 89

This is clearly the ancestor of the modern boiled fig (or plum) pudding, but less rich and far simpler to make.

Fig Pudding

4 oz (1/2 cup) ground blanched almonds
1/2 cup water
1/2 cup white wine (or, for a stronger flavour, madeira)
1 cup dried figs, cut into quarters and any stems removed
1 cup seeded (or seedless) raisins, whole
2 tbsp clear honey
1/2 tsp ginger
1/4 tsp salt

Mix the ground almonds into a paste in a saucepan with some of the wine and/or water, over medium heat; add rest of

liquid and allow to steep a few minutes over low heat while you cut up the figs. Stir in fruits and all seasonings and bring to a boil; cook, stirring, for about 5 minutes, or until the mixture is thick and well blended. Serve warm. If you wish to do this ahead of time, put the pudding in an ovenproof dish and cover it with foil, to be reheated in the oven.

116 Tartys in Applis

𝔗ak gode Applys and gode Spycis and 𝔉igys and reysons and Perys and wan they are well ybrayed coloure wyth Safron wel and do yt in a cofyn, and do yt forth to bake wel.

AC II:23

Another similar recipe calls for prunes in place of figs, and directs that the fruits be minced rather than ground. Other variations occur in the second recipe (and elsewhere); our compromise here is the simplest version. The quantity is for a fairly large tart (ca 9-10 inches).

Apple Tarts

ca 2 lbs tart apples
optional: 1-2 very firm pears may be substituted for some of
  the apples, but not all varieties of pears are suitable: avoid
  Bartlett pears, which are too soft when they are ripe
ca 1/2 cup dried figs or prunes, stoned and chopped
1/3 cup raisins
1/2 cup sugar (brown, white, or a combination)
1/4 tsp each cinnamon, nutmeg, mace, salt
1/8 tsp ground cloves
pinch saffron
pastry for one pie shell

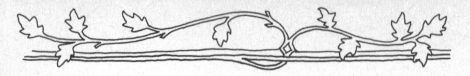

Peel and core apples (and pears, if used) and chop: pieces must be much smaller than the slices used in a normal apple pie today. Or, put all the fruit (fresh and dried) through the coarse blade of a meat grinder. Put the fruits in prepared pastry shell; mix sugar and spices and spread them over. Cover the tart with a sheet of aluminum foil; bake about 45 minutes at 375°, removing foil cover towards end of cooking time.

VARIATIONS

For a firmer filling, add up to 1/4 cup (2 oz) of ground almonds, dissolved in an equal quantity of water, plus (if you wish) 2 tbsp cooking oil. Or, for a 'flaune of Almayne' (Arundel), add cream beaten with eggs, and some butter.

117 𝔖ambocade

𝔗ake & make a 𝔠rust in a trap & take crudded and wryng out þe wheyȝe, and drawe hem þurgh a strynor, and put in the strynor crusts. 𝔇o þerto suger the þridde part & somdel whyte of Ayren, & shake þerin bloms of elren, & bake it up with curose & mess it forth. FC 171

Elders are generally in bloom in late June and/or early July; their blossoms make a very nice flavouring for this simple cheese pie.

Elderflower Cheese Pie

pastry to line a pie dish
12 oz cottage cheese, drained of any watery whey
1/2 cup sugar
1/2 cup (or less, if bread is stale enough to make very fine
   crumbs) white bread crumbs
4 egg whites
ca 1/2 cup elder blossoms (3-4 clusters)

Leave your elder sprays in a glass of water until the crust is prepared: the blossoms are apt to discolour slightly if prepared too far in advance. When you are ready to prepare the filling, carefully strip off the white blossoms, trying not to include the little green stems. Then beat cottage cheese, sugar, crumbs, and egg whites together: a blender is ideal for the purpose. When this mixture is smooth, stir in the blossoms and pour the filling into the prepared shell. Bake about 45 minutes in a 350° oven. The pie is excellent either hot or cold.

118 𝔇arpoles

𝕿ake 𝕮reme of 𝕮owe mylke, oþer of 𝔄lmandſ; do þerto apren with ſuger, ſafron, and ſalt; medle it pfere; do it in a coffyn of ii. ynche depe; bake it wel and ſerue it forth.

FC 183

Custard Tarts

pastry to make an open pie shell or 12 tart shells
2 cups light cream, or a combination of cream and milk
4 eggs (or 8 egg yolks, if you prefer)
1/2 cup sugar
1/4 tsp salt
optional: pinch ground saffron (for colour); 1/4 tsp almond
    extract or a pinch each ground cloves, ginger, mace (or
    other spices: nutmeg and cinnamon, for example); or
    1/2-1 cup chopped dates or other dried fruit, or fresh
    strawberries

Beat eggs and sugar together, and then beat in cream and seasonings. Pour into prepared pie shell or tart shells, over fruit (if fruit is used). For one large tart, bake 10 minutes at 450°,

then about 30 at 300°-325°; for small tarts, about 20 minutes at 400°.

VARIATIONS

1 Custard Lumbarde: add prunes and dates (both cut up) to the basic mixture.

2 Cheese Daryoles: substitute drained cottage cheese, or a combination of dry cottage cheese (forced through a sieve, unless you are using a blender) with sour cream, for the cream, and use only 3 eggs or 6 egg yolks. Do not mix in spices, but sprinkle a bit of nutmeg and cinnamon over the top. This can be highly recommended to lovers of cheesecake.

119 Fretoure

Take whete Floure, Ale, ȝest, Safroun, & Salt, & bete alle togederys as þikke as þou schuldyst make oþer bature in fleyssche tyme, & þan take fayre Applys, & kut hem in maner of Fretourys, & wete hem in þe bature vp on downne, & frye hem in fayre Oyle, & caste hem in a dyssche, & caste Sugre þer=on & serue forth.

HARL 279.II.54

This recipe has the advantage of being a yeast recipe which calls for no special skill in handling yeast doughs; nor are skills in deep-fat frying necessary – the fritters may be cooked in a small amount of oil and turned over to brown both sides, if preferred. The flavour is very interesting indeed, too.

Apple Fritters

1 package dry yeast
1 1/4 cup ale or beer

1 cup flour
2 egg yolks or 1 egg
3-4 apples (Macintosh, for example, are suitable)
1/2 tsp salt
oil or shortening for frying

Heat the beer to lukewarm. Put the yeast in a medium-sized mixing bowl and add 1/4 cup of the beer; stir and let it sit for about 10 minutes. Then add flour, egg yolks or egg, salt, and remaining beer. Beat the mixture together, then cover the bowl and let it sit in a warm place (such as the back of the stove, while you use the front burners to cook the rest of the meal) for about an hour. It should at least double in bulk. Then peel the apples, core them, and cut in wedges. Put apple slices in the bowl of batter and stir to coat apples with batter. Fry quickly in oil or deep fat; drain the browned fritters on paper as you remove them from the pan. When all have been cooked, sprinkle with sugar and serve. To prepare ahead of time, simply be sure not to overcook; reheat for a few minutes in a moderate oven, and add the sugar just before serving.

VARIATION

A non-Lenten version calls for milk, rather than ale, omits yeast, and seasons with pepper and saffron. Aside from the pepper, this means something corresponding to more modern recipes for the dish, and we do not think it as interesting. The batter may also be simply flour and egg.

120 Rapeye

Take dow, & make þer-of a þinne kake; þanne take Fygys & raysonys smal y-grounde, & temper hem with Almaunde Milke; take pouder of Pepir, & of Galyngale, Clowes, & menge to-gederys, & ley on þin kake a-long as bene koddys; & ober-caste þin kake to-gederys, & dewte on þe eggys, an frye in Oyle, & serue forth. HARL 279.II.47

Dumplings of Dried Fruit in Paste

4 dried figs
1/2 cup raisins
1 tbsp ground almonds
1 tbsp hot water
1/8 tsp each ground pepper, galingale (or ginger), cloves
fresh noodles, rolled very thin and cut in pieces 3-4 inches
    long and 1 1/2-2 inches wide; or ready-made eggroll paste,
    cut in two lengthwise

Mix the hot water and ground almonds. Let them stand while you put the figs and raisins through a food grinder. Add the almond mixture and spices to the figs and raisins; mix thoroughly. Put a thin line of the fruit mixture down the centre of the pieces of dough. Moisten the edges with egg. Fold over lengthwise, so the paste encloses the fig mixture in a long, narrow case, similar in shape to a bean pod. Deep fry and serve.

VARIATION
Risshewes is a similar recipe. The filling includes figs, pine-nuts, currants, dates, sugar, saffron, ginger, and salt. These are enclosed in a thin paste made with flour, sugar, and salt, and then deep fried.

121 Cryspez

Take Whyte of Eyroun, Mylke, & Floure, & a lytel Berme, & bete it to-gederys, & draw it þorw a straynoure, so þat it be renneng, & not to styf, & caste Sugre þer-to, & Salt; þanne take a chafer ful of freyssche grece boyling, & put þin hond in þe Bature, & lat þin bature renne dowun by þin fyngerys in-to þe chafere; & whan it is ronne to-gedere on þe chafere, & is y-now, take & nym a skymer, & take it vp, & lat al þe grece renne owt, & put it on a fayre dyssche, & cast þer-on Sugre y-now, & serue forth. HARL 4016

Not all recipes for this dish call for yeast, and some appear to indicate something closer to a modern crêpe: those who wish to make the pancake type should see the variation below, but the more usual cryspez, given here are very good indeed.

Crisps

1/2 cup milk
1/2 tsp yeast (granular)
1 egg white
1/2 cup flour
2 tbsp sugar
dash salt

Dissolve the yeast in warm milk. Beat the other ingredients together (a wire whisk is best) and beat in yeast mixture; the batter should be runny. Fry in deep fat, dribbling the batter in with a spoon or fingers (as the original recipe suggests). Turn when browned on the bottom. Remove with a skimmer or slotted spoon and drain on absorbent paper. Sprinkle with sugar, or shake in a bag with the sugar. Some recipes say to 'serve them forth with fritters,' which they closely resemble; they could be mixed with apple fritters – see recipe for Fretoure (119).

VARIATION
The Ménagier's recipe calls for whole eggs, flour, salt, water, and wine, beaten together; this mixture is to be fried, preferably in butter, poured in so that it 'runs all around the pan' – which sounds like a way of making a single, thin pancake. This can be done successfully using about the same proportions as a modern French crêpe: eg, to a cup of flour, 2 eggs, 1/2 cup each water and white wine, and ca 1/4 tsp salt. Such crêpes may be served as a dessert course, with sugar sprinkled on (as the Ménagier recommends), or served rolled around a runny filling, such as Mawmenny (85).

122 Gyngere Brede

Take a quart of hony, & sethe it, & skeme it clene; take Safroun, pouder Pepir, & prow þer=on; take gratyd Brede, & make it so chargeaunt þat it wol be y=lechyd; þen take pouder Canelle, & straw þer=on y=now; þen make þit square lyke as þou wolt leche yt; take when þou lechyst hyt, and caste Box leves a=bouen, y=styked þer=on, clowys. And ȝif þou wolt haue it Red, coloure it with Saunderys y=now.

HARL 279.II.4

Do not expect this gingerbread to resemble its modern spice-cake descendant. Both texture and flavour will be quite different, though equally delicious. But we must make up for the absent-mindedness of the scribe who neglected to tell us when to add ginger.

Gingerbread

1/2 cup clear honey
1 loaf bread (1 lb), at least 4 days old, grated or ground into fine crumbs; if bread is too fresh, it will not make sufficiently fine crumbs.
1 tsp each ginger, cinnamon
1/8 tsp ground white pepper
pinch saffron, if desired: it is not important here

Bring the honey to a boil and skim off any scum. Keeping the pan over very low heat, stir in breadcrumbs and spices. When it is a thick, well-blended mass, press firmly into a small greased (or teflon-lined) layer cake pan (8" is ideal for this quantity). Cover and leave in a cool place several hours or overnight before turning out on a cake plate. Cut into small slices to serve.

123 Cybele

Nym almandes, Sugur & salt, & payn de mayn, & bray hem in a morter; do therto eyren; frie hit in oylle or in grece; cast thereto sugur, & 3if hit forth. LAUD 553

This sounds like a recipe for one good-sized cake, but it seems to work better as small cakes – which are more often specified by menus of the period.

Almond Cakes

1 cup (or more: depending on the freshness of the bread)
  breadcrumbs
4 oz (1/2 cup) ground almonds
1/4 cup plus 2 tbsp sugar
1/2 tsp salt
2 eggs
oil and/or fat for frying

Mix dry ingredients (reserving the extra sugar), preferably in a blender; add eggs, beaten, if not using a blender. Heat oil and/or other fat in a frying pan and drop the batter in in small spoonfuls, flattening with the spoon if necessary (which it will not be if you are using deep fat). Turn over once if not using deep fat. Drain on paper, and sprinkle with reserved sugar before serving – warm, preferably.

An alternative procedure which may be convenient and offers good results is to chill the batter for an hour or so, then divide it into balls (about twenty) and flatten into cakes; the cakes should be small and not too thick. One advantage is that much of the work can be done ahead of serving time; another is that the cakes will be of more uniform size, and less uneven in appearance.

124 Payn Pur-dew

Take fapre zolkes of Eproun, & trpe hem fro þe whpte, &
draw hem þorw a strapnoure, & take Salt and caste þer-to;
þan take fapre brede, & kutte it as troundeȝ rounde; þan
take fapre Boter þat is clarpfipd, or ellps fapre Frepsshe
grece, & putte it on a potte, & make it hote; þan take &
wete wpl þin troundeȝ in þe zolkps, & putte hem in þe
panne, and so frpe hem vppe; but ware of cleupng to the
panne; & whan it is frpid, lep hem on a dpsshe, & lep
Sugre p-nowe þer-on, & þanne serue it forth.

HARL 279.II.43

This is a medieval version of what we call French toast, but it
is richer – and if made with good French bread, of a more interesting texture. Those who hesitate to use all those yolks
can substitute whole eggs (half as many) for some or all of
the yolks.

Smothered Bread

8 slices (3/4-1 inch thick) French bread, crusts removed
12 egg yolks, beaten
1/4 tsp salt
1/2 cup sugar (light brown will do: the recipe does not
   specify white)
butter for frying: at least 3 tbsp, more if needed

Heat the butter in a frying pan, but do not allow to burn. Dip
the bread slices in the beaten yolks (or put them in a baking
pan in which they will barely fit and pour the egg yolks over
them, turning, and allowing the egg to soak in a bit while you
are heating the butter). Fry until golden brown on each side,
turning carefully and adding more butter as needed. Put on a
serving platter and sprinkle the sugar over the slices; serve hot.

125 Payn Ragon

Take hony sugar and clarifie it togydre and boile it with esy fyr, and kepe it wel from brenyng and whan it hath yboiled a while, take up a drope þer-of wiþ þy fynger and do it in a litel water and loke if it hong togyder, and take it fro the fyre and do þerto the thriddendele and powdor gyngen and stere it togyder til it bigynne to thik and cast it on a wete table; lesh it and serue it forth with fryed mete on flesh day or on fysshe dayes. FC 67

This recipe makes a fudge-type candy, complete with softball test. The unspecified ingredient added during the beating stage would most probably be ground almonds, currants, pine nuts – the sort of ingredient used to stuff roasts, flavour stews, etc. Pegge suggests that the 'third part' must be bread ('payn'), but it seems more likely that this is one of the names which suggests an appearance rather than an ingredient. Just as 'yrchouns' are sausage made to look like hedgehogs, this is a sweet shaped and sliced like bread. Since this dish is recommended to accompany fried meat, it would provide the kind of contrast that a sweet sauce might.

Honey and Almond Candy

2 cups sugar
3 tbsp honey
2/3 cup water
2/3 cup ground almonds
1/4-1/2 tsp ginger

Cook the sugar, honey, and water together, stirring frequently, over fairly low heat, stirring, until the syrup reaches the softball stage (approximately 234°). Cool it a little, then beat it until it begins to stiffen. Then add the almonds and ginger, stir together, and pour out onto waxed paper. When hardened, slice and serve.

126 Wafers

Wafers are made in five ways. By one method you beat the eggs in a bowl, then add salt and wine and throw in flour, and mix them; then put them on two irons, little by little, each time as much paste as the size of a slice or strip of cheese, and press them between the two irons and cook on both sides. MP

A krumcake iron is necessary to produce anything resembling a medieval wafer; these are available at many specialty kitchen shops, especially in areas where there are Scandinavian cooks. A modern waffle iron is too large to produce a thin wafer, but may be resorted to if you have no other recourse. Cheese is added in two of the Ménagier's five ways.

Wafers

2 eggs
1/4 cup flour
3 tbsp grated cheese (parmesan is fine)
1 tbsp sherry
1/2 tsp salt

Mix all ingredients together (but do not try to beat until light). Put by teaspoons onto krumcake iron and cook on both sides. They will come out on the limp side and need to dry: it is advisable to put them into a low oven to crisp them.

127 Ypocras

Treys Unces de canell, & iij unces de gyngener, spykenard de Spayn le pays dun deners: garyngale, clowes, gylofre, poiurs long, noiez mugadez, maziozame, cardemonii—de chescun quarter douce, grayne de paradys, floer de queynel—de chescun di unce; de toutes soit fait powdor &. FC 191

This Anglo-Norman recipe at least has the virtue of suggesting proportions: otherwise, it is not very clear. Comparison with a number of other recipes makes it clear that the essential ingredients are cinnamon, ginger, sugar, and red wine; the spices are to be mixed with hot wine, then strained. A problem is that the spice powder is very difficult to strain out: if an absolutely clear drink is desired, this must be done over a long period of time using cloth or filter paper. (Or, the mixture may be siphoned out.) This is an after-dinner wine, *not* a table wine. In medieval times it was served with wafers after the meal; it makes a very pleasant post-prandial drink.

Spiced Wine

3 bottles red wine: use *vin ordinaire*; that is, the cheapest red wine you can get that does not have a positively unpleasant taste that even the spices cannot mask
3/4 cup sugar
3 tbsp honey
1/4 cup cinnamon
2 tbsp ginger and/or galingale
1 tsp each nutmeg, mace, cardamom
1/2 tsp ground cloves

Heat the wine, and stir in sugar, honey, and spices, mixed into a paste with a little of the wine, over low heat. Stir until thoroughly dissolved, but avoid boiling. Let sit for a few minutes before straining through a fine mesh strainer. Repeat in a few minutes when wine has had time to settle a bit again. Then funnel into wine bottles and replace caps or corks.

Serve at room temperature.

VARIATIONS

Some recipes suggest a higher proportion of ginger (including the one given above), and some may wish to try a mixture of that sort; we have preferred to follow the advice of the majority of recipes, including those of the Ménagier, which call for a predominence of cinnamon and sugar. Other spices, such as galingale, may be added, but most of those called for are a bit mystifying. Sometimes 'tornsole' is called for; it is a vegetable dye added for colour rather than flavour. We have not tried gillyflower or spikenard because we do not have any, but perhaps others who are provided with these herbs may wish to try them.

A method not suggested in any medieval source, but which is easy and may appeal to those who prefer a clearer look to their ypocras, is to boil the spices whole, as for a modern hot punch, then strain them out.

On Subtleties

Bibliography

Glossary

Index

On Subtleties

While the term 'subtlety' can be applied to virtually any ingenious device or contrivance, in cookery it usually refers to an elaborate edible construction. The most notable exception occurs at the beginning of the *Liber Cure Cocorum*, where the ingenuity is directed towards practical jokes in the kitchen. We are given directions for making cooked meat appear to be raw, for making a pot boil over uncontrollably (by adding soap), and for making meat appear to be full of worms. We do not recommend any of these 'sly3tes of cure' for presentation at a feast, but they do share with more decorative subtleties the characteristic of a deceptive appearance, seeming to be other than what they are; and that is the essence of a subtlety. Though the most common festive subtlety is a representation in sugar of persons or objects, some were made of pastry or even of ground meat. Consider the recipe from *The Forme of Cury* for a pastry castle.

CHASTLETS. Take and make a foyle of gode past with a roller of a foot brode, & lynger by cumpas. Make iiii Coffyns of þe self past uppon þe rollers þe gretnesse of þe smale of þyn Arme, of vi ynche depnesse; make þe gretust in þe myddell. Fasten þe foile in þe mouth upwarde, & fasten þree oþer foure in euery syde. Kerue out keyntlich kyrnels above in þe maner of bataiwyng and drye hem harde in an Ovene, oþer in þe Sunne.

This castle has a huge pork pie for the central tower and the four smaller towers filled with almond cream, custard, ground fruit, etc; however, we feel that it is more practical to make a smaller unfilled version. The most satisfactory we have tried uses a cheese pastry, four round towers, and a square central section.

2 cups flour	1/2 oz each grated parmesan,
1/4 cup shortening	grated cheddar
1/4 cup butter	water

Blend the fat with the flour; add the grated cheese, mix thoroughly, and add water to make a pastry the consistency of pie crust. Divide the dough into five roughly equal portions. Roll each portion into a thin rectangle, approximately 6" x 8". Trim four of them evenly to fit the forms described below, and cut crenelations into one long side. They are now ready to mould into the shape of the four towers. To make these towers, we used the cardboard tube around which wrapping paper, aluminum foil, etc, is wrapped. Ours were 1 3/4" in diameter and 4 1/2" long. You can also make a cylinder from lightweight cardboard. Cover each tube in aluminum foil, butter it lightly, and wrap the pastry around, overlapping and sealing the edges with eggwhite or water.

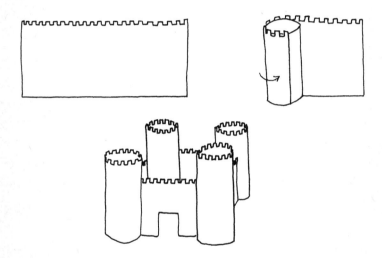

Prick the pastry with a fork so that it will not puff too much. Stand the towers upright on a cookie sheet, and bake at 350°–400° until lightly browned. Then carefully remove the cardboard centre and allow the towers to cool. The fifth portion of pastry is cut into four equal pieces to form the walls between the towers, each approximately 3" high and 2-4" long. Cut crenelations, prick with a fork, and cook flat on a cookie sheet until the pastry is lightly browned. When all the pieces are cooled, join them together, using eggwhite, flour and water paste, or a soft cheese like Brie as glue. The castle is an

158 attractive centrepiece for a medieval table, and (if you can induce your guests to break it up at the end of the feast) it serves as a delicious conclusion to the feast.

More elaborate subtleties, and those designed for specific feast days, are usually constructed of icing made of stiffly beaten eggwhite and enough powdered sugar to make the icing firm enough to hold its shape after being forced through decorator tips. One such subtlety, which could be made by a relatively inexperienced cook, would be a Christmas tree. The first step is to make a cardboard cone the size and shape you want for the tree. Cover the cone with waxed paper. Make eggwhite icing and colour most of it green with food colouring. Starting at the bottom of the cone, force icing through an icing tip in loops (we use the leaf tip for this), gradually working your way to the top of the cone in slightly overlapping loops. Then use a flower tip to place 'decorations' on the tree in whatever colours you choose.

Leave the tree to dry for a day or two: this icing gets very hard, and the longer you can leave it the better. Then remove first the cone from inside the waxed paper and then the paper itself from the hardened icing shape. You can model a large star or angel to attach to the top of the tree with a little icing; icing will keep for days in the refrigerator in a sealed container. To mould a tiny angel, the icing must be very stiff so it can be moulded like clay.

We have used this icing and this basic technique to make very complicated subtleties. One of these was for a feast on St

Juliana's Day. It showed the saint in her prison with the devil looking on. The devil was modeled of icing brought to a clay-like consistency by the addition of extra icing sugar; the saint was constructed on a narrow cardboard cone (with head and hands modeled separately and allowed to dry several days in advance). The prison wall was made on a cardboard frame, with the frame removed when the icing had dried. The whole structure was placed on the bottom of a lightweight cardboard box, with the interior of the prison represented by light gray icing, with lines drawn to represent stones. The exterior of the prison wall had vines with little roses, and green icing represented grass on the base.

The curved wall was strong enough to be anchored with the frosting, which dried and held it firmly in place. Similarly, Juliana's cone-form was held in place by having the edges of her dress trailing on the floor-icing. The devil was constructed with toothpicks protruding from his legs, so that he could be held in place by sticking them through the base and resting one arm against the prison wall. The first step in the construction of the subtlety was to make the devil, the hands and head of the saint, and the prison wall. Next, the prison wall was removed from the form and the concave face (smooth from contact with the waxed paper over the cardboard) was covered in icing with lines drawn to look like stone. Then the saint's body was made, the head and hands attached, and the whole allowed to dry. Next Juliana's hair was put on, using a very fine line tip, and her face painted. Finally the prison wall was put in place, with green icing outside and gray stone icing inside; the saint was put in place; holes were punched for the toothpicks and the devil put in place. The whole contruction was allowed to dry for several days before it was transported to the feast.

Be sure to allow enough time for complicated subtleties, and for experimentation when you are confronted with a difficult design. Every step of construction should be planned in advance, with plenty of time for drying – extra time may be required if something breaks or simply does not look right. Colour the icing *before* moulding faces, flowers, trees, walls, etc. You may wish to paint pinker cheeks with water colour or dilute food colouring when a head is dry, but an attempt to colour subtleties entirely by painting white icing is streaky, mottled, and generally unsatisfactory. Make duplicates of difficult or fragile parts – heads, wings, walls, etc – so that you can choose the best, and so that no time will be lost if something breaks. Allow at least two or three days for the whole construction to dry before the feast, but not months: the colours fade over a long period. Move the subtlety at least five or six hours in advance to the place where the feast will be held so that there will be time to make repairs if it breaks in transit. Reserve a small amount of icing to use in such repairs. It would be best for the aspiring subtlety-maker to begin with a relatively simple project: the Christmas tree, or a pastry or icing castle, for example. Before attempting a complicated combination of figures, try making a single human form. The complexity of the final production depends on the time, ingenuity, and ability of the subtlety-maker; with practice, almost anything can be attempted with pleasing results.

Bibliography

Aebischer, Paul 'Un manuscrit valaisan du "Viandier" attribué
à Taillevent' *Vallesia* 8 (Sion 1953) 73-100. Contains a very
early ms of the *Viandier*, which is usually dated ca 1380;
however, Aebischer gives evidence that this ms can be no
later than 1320, and concludes that Taillevent (qv below)
simply gave out his own version of an already established
text.

Anderson, John L., ed *A Fifteenth Century Cookry Boke*
(New York 1962). A handsomely illustrated selection from
the recipes printed by Austin (qv below), with an unusually
full glossary of cooking term; useful, if sometimes of questionable accuracy and rather flip in tone.

Aresty, Esther B. *The Delectable Past* (New York 1964). As
its very long subtitle indicates, this book runs the gamut
from ancient Greece to the late nineteenth century. The
brief section on medieval food contains a few rather drastically 'adapted' recipes.

Austin, Thomas, ed *Two Fifteenth Century Cookery Books*
EETS os 91 (London 1888). The two 'cookery books' meant
by the title are mss Harl 279 (ca 1430) and 4016 (ca 1450),
but Austin also includes parts of Ashmole 1439, Laud 553,
and Douce 55. The most generally available large collection
of fifteenth century recipes, this also contains some feast
menus of the period and other interesting information.

Barber, Richard *Cooking and Recipes from Rome to the
Renaissance* (London 1973). Barber's documentation is
sparse and he does not give his recipes in the original, only
his own adaptations; however, he gives much information –
usually if not invariably sound – and his recipes are usable.
About half the book (63 pp) is devoted to medieval food.

Buttes, Henry *Dyets Dry Dinner* (London 1599). Contains
many recipes almost (or entirely) identical to those of a
hundred or more years before.

162 Carter, Charles *The Compleat City and Country Cook, or, Accomplish'd Housewife* (2nd ed London 1736). Even in this eighteenth century work, much can be found that echoes or illuminates medieval recipes. The newer dishes represented here are more complicated and difficult.

Digby, Kenelm *The Closet of the Eminently Learned Sir Kenelme Digbie Kt. Opened, Published by his Son's Consent* (London 1669). Another indication that medieval cooking habits were flourishing in the seventeenth century, this makes amusing reading, for we are continually being informed of the culinary practices of various lords and ladies.

Furnivall, Frederick J., ed *The Babee's Book* EETS os 32 (London 1868, repr New York 1969). Contains several books on manners, with emphasis on table manners, and other matters relating to medieval food, including the *Modus Cenandi*, the *Bokes of Nurture* of Hugh Rhodes and John Russell, Wynkyn de Worde's *Boke of Kervynge*, and a number of Latin graces, as well as two pages of recipes. Almost all the material here is fifteenth century, but the editor did not always indicate dates.

The Good Hus-wifes Handmaide for the Kitchen (London 1594). Among the recipes which are versions of earlier ones is an informative version of chicken cooked with marrowbones and served with 'brewes.'

Lodge, Barton, ed *Palladius on Husbondrie* EETS os 52 (London 1873). A fifteenth century English ms translated from a Latin one written in Italy, this lists many vegetables which do not appear in menus or recipes of the period, such as asparagus, but which must have been known in England since their names appear in distinctly English forms.

Maino de' Maineri *De saporibus* ed Lynn Thorndike 'A Medieval Sauce-Book' *Speculum* 9 (1934) 183-90. Fourteenth century Italian versions of recipes found in English and French mss.

Markham, Gervase *The English Housewife* (London 1649). Another seventeenth century collection which contains instructive versions of medieval dishes such as chicken boiled with marrowbones and gingerbread.

Mead, William Edward *The English Medieval Feast* (1931,
repr New York 1967). The standard and most informative
work on English food and its preparation and service in the
period, but one must put up with the author's lack of sym-
pathy with his subject, imprecise documentation, and some
outright errors. Still very useful, but to be handled with care.
*Le Ménagier de Paris, composé vers 1393 par un Bourgeois
Parisien* ed Jérôme Pichon (2 vols, Paris 1896). The standard, complete edition of the most illuminating book from
medieval France. The second volume is almost entirely devoted to matters culinary.
Morris, R., ed *Liber Cure Cocorum* (London 1862). An early
fifteenth century collection of recipes given in doggerel
verse.
Napier, Mrs Alexander [Robina], ed *A Noble Boke of
Cookry ffor a Prynce Houssolde or eny other Estately
Houssolde* (London 1882). Prints a fifteenth century ms
from the Holkham collection.
Pegge, Samuel, ed *The Forme of Cury* (London 1780). The
title collection is attributed on the first page of the ms to
'the chef Maister cokes of kyng Richard the Secunde,' an
attribution no one has doubted; it has been dated 1390.
The volume also contains another late fourteenth century
roll, the two-part 'Ancient Cookery.'
Power, Eileen, trans *The Goodman of Paris* (London 1928).
An abridged translation of the *Ménagier de Paris*; unfortu-
nately, it contains fewer than half the recipes.
Sass, Lorna J. *To the King's Taste: Richard II's Book of
Feasts and Recipes Adapted for Modern Cooking* (New
York: Metropolitan Museum of Art 1975). This adaptation
of the *Forme of Cury* is actually a selection (40 recipes; the
entire collection is 196), including some not from FC. It has
a strong preponderance of sweet, spicy, or 'odd' dishes and
is often rather freely adapted: sometimes downright wrong,
as is the case with the first recipe. But it has some interesting dishes we have not included, much information about
medieval kitchens and serving habits, an interesting bibliography, and other worthwhile apparatus. We cannot agree

164   with many of the pronouncements made about spices, for
reasons sketched above in our introduction.

Serjeantson, M.S. 'The Vocabulary of Cookery in the Fifteenth Century' in *Essays and Studies by Members of the
English Association* 23 (1937) 25-37. A valuable check-list
of cooking terms, though not always absolutely reliable; like
others, the author tended to jump to conclusions about
spices on insufficient evidence.

Simon, André L. *Guide to Good Foods and Wines* (rev ed
London 1963). A good source of information about cooking
terms, techniques, and ingredients which may be unusual today.

Taillevent *Le Viandier de Guillaume Tirel dit Taillevent* ed
Jérôme Pichon and George Vicaire (Paris 1892). A standard
fourteenth century work, drawing upon the same sources as
the Ménagier, but often rather more confused (and confusing) than the latter. It is attributed to a master cook of the
French royal kitchens of about the same time as FC.

Tannahill, Reay *Food in History* (London 1973). A survey
running from pre-historic times to the nineteenth century,
with primary emphasis on why people ate what they did in
various times and places. The sections on the middle ages
are limited but informative.

Warner, Richard, ed *Antiquitates Culinariae: Tracts on Culinary Affairs of the Old English* (London 1791). An edition
of FC and other mss, including Arundel.

Wilson, C. Anne *Food and Drink in Britain* (London 1973).
A very thorough and informative survey, well documented.

Wright, Thomas, ed *A Volume of Vocabularies* ([England]
1857). Contains Alexander Neckham's twelfth century re-
marks on matters culinary.

Cosman, Madeleine P. *Fabulous Feasts: Medieval Cookery
and Ceremony* (New York 1976). 'Popular'; illustrated; no
sources for recipes which appear to be free adaptations.

Henish, Bridget Ann *Fast and Feast: Food in Medieval
Society* (University Park 1976). Interesting and scholarly
discussion of medieval attitudes to preparation and presentation of food. Carefully documented.

Glossary

These are common terms; those which appear less frequently, or which should be easily understood, are not included, nor are all the variant spellings. Those who wish to consult more complete glossaries should check the bibliography.

ALAY, ALYE, LYE mix, dilute
AMYDON, AMYDONE, AMYNDOUN
  a wheat starch
ARAY dress, decorate

BRAY grind, crush
BROCCHE spit
BRUET sauce, broth

CANEL, CANELLE, CANNELL
  cinnamon
CAST add
CAWDEL thick soup or sauce
CHARGEANT thick
COFYN, COFFYN pastry shell
COLE usually strain, but some-
  times cool
COMYN (n) cumin
CONEY, CONNYNGE, CONY
  rabbit
COUCHE, COWCHE lay, arrange

DO: + ÞERTO add; + THEREABOVE
  pour over; + YT put it
DRAWE UP or THERTO mix with a
  liquid
DELE part

EYREN, EYROUN, AYREN,
  HEYREYN eggs

FARS mixture of ground
  ingredients
FLE flay, remove skin
FLOER, FLOWER, FLOWR (n)
  flour or flower
FLOER, FLORISSH (vb) decorate,
  garnish
FOIL, FOYLE leaf, often of
  rolled pastry
FORCE, FORS stuff or season
  (cf FARS)

GALYNTYN, GALYNTYNE spices,
  sometimes with breadcrumbs,
  as for a Pike in Galentine
GELOFLOR, GELOFRE, GILOFRE
  'gillyflower,' but almost always
  means 'cloves,' even in the
  phrase 'cloves of gilofre'
GREDERN gridiron

HELDE pour; Y-HELID covered
HEWE cut, chop

ICORNE, ICORUE cut (carved) up

KELE cool

LECHE, LESH, LESHE slice
LICOUR, LYCOUR, LYKOURE liquid

LIRE, LIORE, LYRE flesh
LYOR, LYOS, LYRE mixture
(see also LIRE)

MEDEL, MEDLE, MELLE mix;
sometimes, serve
MENGE, MYNG mix, mix in
MYLK, MYLKE unless cow's milk
('mylk of kyne,' eg) is specified,
ground almonds mixed with a
liquid

NENE, NYM take

OÞ, OÞER, OÞÞER or; sometimes,
other

PAST pastry
POSSYNET pan for sautéing or
stewing
POUDER, POWDER (etc) ground
spices; + DOUCE mild spices;
+ FORT strong spices

QUIBIBES, QUYBIBES cubebs

RAYSONS, REYSEYNS (etc) [of]
CORANCE, CORANTE (etc)
currants
RENNENG thin, runny, liquid

SANDERS, SAUNDERYS, SAUNDERS
sandalwood or red cedar, used
for colouring

SEETH, SEEÞ, SEÞE, SITH simmer
or boil (except in 77: 'after-
wards')
SEW, SEWE, SOWE broth, sauce
SIRIP, SIRRIPPE broth, sauce
SODEN, SOÞE, YSODE boiled; past
tense of SEETHE
STEPE steep, soak
STOCKFISH (variously spelled)
dried salt cod or similar fish
STONDYNG stiff, very thick
STREYNOUR strainer; 'wryng' or
'drawe' through a strainer:
beat, strain, pulverize
SWYNG beat

TEMPER, TEMPUR dilute, mix
TRAP baking dish

VERGEOUS, VERJUICE, VERIOUS
tart fruit juice, usually made
from grape juice too sour for
wine or from crabapples; the
Ménagier suggests bitter orange
juice as a substitute, which is
close to the lemon we generally
use

WASTEL, WASTREL white bread

YFERE, IN FERE together
YNOGH, Y-NOUHZ, YNOW enough;
done; or, nearly done

Index

Middle English titles (or translated French ones) are indicated by bold type. Sub-entries are indicated by italic. All numbers are recipe numbers.